The Audition Sourcebook

Do's, Don'ts,
and an Online Guide to 2,100+
Monologues and Musical Excerpts

Randall Richardson
and
Don Sandley

HEINEMANN
Portsmouth, NH

Heinemann
A division of Reed Elsevier Inc.
361 Hanover Street
Portsmouth, NH 03801–3912
www.heinemanndrama.com

Offices and agents throughout the world

Library of Congress Cataloging-in-Publication Data
Richardson, Randall.
   The audition sourcebook : do's, don'ts, and an online guide to 2,100+ monologues and musical excerpts / Randall Richardson and Don Sandley.
      p. m.
   Includes bibliographical references.
   ISBN 0-325-00335-1
   1. Musicals—Auditions. 2. Acting—Auditions. 3. Popular music—Bibliography. 4. Monologues—Bibliography. I. Sandley, Don. II. Title.

MT956 .R56 2001
792.6'028—dc21

2001024857

Editor: Lisa A. Barnett
Production: Elizabeth Valway
Cover design: Catherine Hawkes, Cat & Mouse Design
Typesetting: Tom Allen
Director of technology: Jeff Northrop
Website development: Harbor Light Productions
Manufacturing: Steve Bernier

Printed in the United States of America on acid-free paper
05 04 03 02 01 DA 1 2 3 4 5

Contents

On the Website
<heinemanndrama.com/auditionsourcebook>
Monologues for Female
   Ancient Greece to Jacobean England
      1500–1800
      1800–1915
      1915–Present
Monologues for Male
   Ancient Greece to Jacobean England
      1500–1800
      1800–1915
      1915–Present
Songs for Soprano
Songs for Mezzo-Soprano/Belter
Songs for Tenor
Songs for Baritone-Bass
Video Demonstrations
   Monologue
   Voice Lesson

Acknowledgments

Writing acknowledgments is like writing an acceptance speech for a Tony. No matter how many people you thank, once you're finished you'll remember someone you left out. With that fact in mind, I'd like to thank the following people: Heinemann's Lisa Barnett for her intuition that this book would be a worthwhile project and for her help in giving it life; Kirstie Carnahan of StrawHat Auditions, Scott Steele of University/Resident Theatre Association, and Southeastern Theatre Conference for their helpfulness in allowing us to observe their auditions, in setting up interviews with theatre directors, and in providing useful information, all of which will always be appreciated; and Lindsey Wallace, my talented voice student, who assisted in the sample voice lesson. Teaching you the past five years has been a joy (and never boring).

I would be remiss if I did not express love and gratitude to my parents, who probably thought I was crazy (but always supported me) when I decided to major in music two weeks before starting college. Thanks also go to Dallas Draper—the greatest voice teacher in the world, my mentor, and a second father to me; to Bruce Kolb, the second greatest voice teacher in the world and a great friend (my time spent in your New York voice studio has been a source of inspiration, both in my teaching and in research for this book); to Wallace McKenzie, who planted the writing seed in me years ago when I was struggling with my doctoral monograph; and to my students, both theatre and music. Teaching you fulfills my life as an educator; I learn as much from you as you do from me.

Last, but most important, is my family, who have put up with my staying at school late, working during vacations, and buying all the musical theatre CDs and vocal selection books in existence. My patient and long-suffering wife, Rebecca, will never know how much I love and treasure her. Colin, my brilliant son, will never know how much I've enjoyed our trips to Germany, our conversations, and his being a student at Samford. Eden, my songbird, will never know how much I enjoy being with her and hearing her sing. If she hadn't been interested in musical theatre, I wouldn't be writing this today. As the least intelligent member of the family, I draw my strength from all of you and will cherish you my entire life.

Randall Richardson

A project like this one inevitably takes more time and effort than we think when the idea originally comes to us. I want to thank my wife, Lynette Moore Sandley, and my daughter, Caitlin Joy Sandley, for sharing me with the book and for the hours and hours of typing they both put in to help me finish. I also wish to thank Rebecca Burroughs for her enthusiastic support of this project and the many hours she spent at the computer keyboard. Ed Landers also has our everlasting gratitude and thanks for his tireless patience and unselfishness in producing the video demonstrations.

These monologues and the techniques discussed in this book are tested in an academic setting with the help and efforts of many college theatre students. I need to acknowledge all the students who have come through my classroom over the years, but I especially want to thank Samford University students Kristen Boutwell, Lorah Bond, Erica Currington, Kelly Dawn Miller, and Stephanie Pela, without whose assistance this book may not have come together.

Finally, I need to thank my colleagues in the Department of Speech Communication and Theatre at Samford University for their tolerance of my emotional outbursts and my disorganization during the writing and research phase of this project. I owe them all lunch.

Don Sandley

Introduction

Don Sandley

People I meet in social settings (social settings that attract nontheatrical types) ask me, "So what do you do . . . exactly?" By this I assume they mean, how do I account for my daily hours, or exactly what do the people who sign my check get from me each day? This question has prompted me to take inventory of my life and work in university theatre. Inevitably, when I think about time and the parsing out of it, I am struck by the vast amount of time spent coaching young actors in the craft of the audition or conducting auditions of my own. The audition is perhaps as artificial and dehumanizing as theatre gets; nonetheless, it consumes a great deal of time and even more mental and emotional energy. This being the case, we feel the need to create a record of our observations on this process in hopes of streamlining the process for others, even taking some of the mystery out of the mayhem. This book can serve as a type of owner's manual for high school, college, and community theatre actors. Professional actors may not find much in this volume that is new. Professionals have learned through experience what this book explores in theory. Some of the suggestions in this book come from professionals who have related their experiences to us. We have arrived at our advice after considering both the stories of success and the anecdotes of failure. Auditioning is not rocket science or the M.S.A.T. The aptitudes it requires are not stressed in the average high school curriculum. In fact, some of the very antics that make for a great audition would ensure your expulsion from any civilized gathering. Most of what we will tell you is just solid practical advice. Some of our information is a marketing strategy—a strategy for marketing yourself. Often you will find yourself saying, "Well, of course, why didn't I think of that?" You probably would have thought about it after fifteen years of coaching auditions, listening to the screeches of joy when a call-board displays a name or the sobs of despair when a name does not appear. As time went by, we began to decipher why some names went up and others did not. The whole process is not so mysterious as it seems. Auditioning is an artificial indicator of talent and a very poor way of conducting employment interviews. Auditioning by cattle call is tantamount to Goldman Sach's hiring investment bankers based on whether or not they wear a red tie to the interview. Sixty seconds and sixteen bars does not reveal anything about whether or not an actor can sustain a two-hour narrative, or develop an emotional bond with other characters, or even if the actor's voice will hold up for a two-show-a-day run. However, auditioning is an established institution and, like many cruel institutions (bullfighting and boxing, for example), auditioning has deep cultural roots and an avid patronage. So, let's get you, the matador, ready for the ring, because if you are going in there, better the bull gets the raw deal than you.

I first discovered how cruel this ritual was when I was an undergraduate in college. As a junior, I was set to audition for *Our Town*, the first main-stage event of the theatrical season. I prepared myself as thoroughly as I knew how in those days, by reading the play over and over and over, reading the criticisms, both literary and theatrical, and locking in on the role I knew I could play. I memorized huge passages of George's dialogue and was set to illuminate the part for the ages.

The morning of the audition, about six-thirty, a knock came at my door. My mother was there to collect me. My grandfather had died in the night, and I had to go to Alabama. Somewhere along the road at a gas station I called the director in desperation and asked for a stay of execution. He said that I could audition late if I returned by a certain date. I was relieved, but my relief was short-lived. When I returned, my audition was a brief sit-down read in the director's office. None of the parts he had me read for were George, and he cast me as Simon Stinson, the town drunk.

In retrospect, I have learned at least three things from this experience. First, all the preparation in the world will not guarantee you the kind of success you want in an audition. You may buy this book, follow our suggestions, and work as hard as any actor ever has and still not even get a callback. However, if you have your heart set on being an actor, whether you are trying for the part of Auntie Mame in your local community theatre or trying to be admitted to an elite acting conservatory, remember: this audition is just *one audition*, and just may be the one before the *right* one. After being cast as Simon in *Our Town*, I was cast (by the same director) in the lead for *The Good Doctor* by Neil Simon, for which I received fine reviews and some awards. Acting is a career for individuals with tunnel vision and the heart to persevere through rejection.

Second, you have to accept that some things are out of your control. One of my students put together a terrific song and monologue package for a large regional audition. She broke through the initial screening audition with ease and was prepared to audition for a large number of potential employing companies. Then her audition number arrived. She was number 591 out of 591. By the time her audition rolled around, she was distraught, frustrated, and resentful. She saw company after company gather up their gear and leave for the airport. Her friends had already received job offers and were basking in the glow of acting utopia. When she walked on to perform her ninety seconds of magic, she hated the remaining casting directors for luring her with false hope and resented me for encouraging her to believe in herself. She received no job offers and was turned off by the process for a long time. Now, what should she have done? As cheesy as it sounds, you have to hope against hope that you will get a fair break and give it all you have. But when the worst-case scenario occurs, accept it. Move on. Your last audition is historical fact; like the assassination of Lincoln or the formation of the Grand Canyon, there is nothing you can do to make it appear different for the record books or to expunge it from your memory. So just learn, laugh, and live. Finally, Simon Stinson was one of my favorite roles. In fact, it is the only part in *Our Town* I can even stomach to think about now. What I learned is this: we do not always know what is best for us as artists. Sometimes our greatest growth, our richest triumph may start out as failure. If you get a chance to act, any part, any time, you have been handed a piece of the purest gold—relish it, adore it, and treat it with the greatest fidelity. The part will be just as kind to you. How do we get the part? That is where we start.

1

What Directors Look For— The Writ of Auditioning Wisdom

Don Sandley

I make my living as a director. I direct professionals, amateurs, and would-be professionals. I do not presume to speak for the College of Directors International, but I know what I look for when I conduct an audition. For me the audition is all about fit. I look for the actors that mesh and hold the promise of an ensemble. The audition is a winnowing process. The entire endeavor is conducted in layers, methodically excluding some and embracing others. The first layer, the cattle call, is the most difficult to survive. For you the actor, this first layer is critical. You must learn the techniques that prove most successful in the first layer, so you can prove later that you are an actor. I give my advice as an ancient holy man might. These shalts and shalt nots are useful for a profitable life in the theatre. These are the Five Commandments of Auditioning. Ten would be just too many. An actor has to have some space for creativity.

The First Commandment—Thou Shalt Choose Thy Material with All Due Care and After Long Hours of Consideration; Once Chosen, Make the Monologue Your Own

This commandment is so important we have dedicated most of the printing budget of this book to suggestions that may help in this research. Choosing the right song for you or the right monologue for you is the absolute, basic necessity for a successful audition.

Choosing the right monologue starts with an honest inventory of your physical and vocal traits. This is the toughest job an actor faces, admitting limitations. Until you have sat in a theatre and listened to a fifty-something gentleman wail the love cries of Romeo or witnessed a maternal forty-something woman reel off "Dance Ten: Looks Three" from *A Chorus Line*, then you do not really understand true social discomfort.

Return for a moment to my audition story from my college days. I wanted the part of George in *Our Town*. I worked hard for the part, even updating my resume for heightened professional effect. None of this could change the fact that I am not the physical type directors look for to play romantic leads like George in *Our Town*. I am five feet seven and have been compared to the late Marty Feldman. In those fanciful days of youth, no one said to me, "Don, take stock of yourself, and choose your aspirations accordingly." I wish someone had. I would have been a lot happier about playing Simon Stinson. I was fortunate to have been cast at all.

Now would be a good time to mention some points that should be obvious but seem to escape the logic of young actors. Consider these points as you look for your monologue.

Shock Is Not a Good Thing

When a director has seen 323 auditionees in two days, the only thing that will shock is a really interesting audition. No string of profanity, no extended recitation on anatomy or violent displays of the psychotic mind can rouse the exhausted casting director from a stupor. The only proverbial Prince Charming kiss available to you is a good piece of literature that creates a story worth hearing from a character worth knowing. I really believe that young actors choose "shock" monologues because they are exploring the outer fringes of their world, those dark and dangerous places your high school director and especially your parents forbade you to visit. Fine art exists in part for just such an exploration. But you wouldn't cover your arms in tattoos and pierce your tongue in preparation for a job interview at a bank. So don't memorize a string of obscenities or practice throwing furniture in preparation to audition for musical theatre or for summer stock theatre or even for community theatre. Demographics prove that primarily women over the age of fifty patronize musical theatre, summer stock theatre, and community theatre. They do not like being shocked and neither do the directors who sell them tickets.

Don't Use a Dialect, Especially a Foreign Dialect

I once sat in an audition and listened to a monologue performed in the most charming Australian dialect I had ever heard. After the audition the actor read the critique form. The three casting critics marked the actor down and did not permit advancement because of the "fake" dialect. It turned out the actor was really from Australia. When confronted with this, the judges simply said they were sorry, but all decisions were final. Now this is an extreme example, but it does display the hostility some directors feel toward unfamiliar dialects. American theatre has a terrible inferiority complex. We have had it for years, and many directors protect the turf by insisting we audition in *American, by-gawd, English*. This may be foolish, it may be provincial, it simply may be the result of years of bad dialect auditions and the unspeakable embarrassment they caused for directors, but you cannot change this reality. Do not try. Just neutralize your good old American dialect and concentrate on homegrown literature, or at least literature you can serve with your native twang.

Do Not Insult, Berate, or Otherwise Incite Your Audition Audience

The choice of material you make for the audition should take into account that your audience does not know the context of the monologue within the play and that some directors view your choice of material as a reflection of your world view. This may not seem fair but it is the way it is. I once saw a young man, who had prepared a monologue from selected slices of the work of Lenny Bruce, audition for the regional level of the Irene

Ryan National Scholarships. The excerpts he had chosen were racist diatribes against African Americans. In the original, Lenny Bruce brought home the point that we all harbor some prejudices, but this young man had edited out the punch line. He entered the hall to perform the audition and realized one of the three critics who would decide his fate on this day was African American. He did not make the semifinals; in fact, he left the event in a sulk. But he had no one to blame except himself and his coach for selecting such a lamebrained audition piece. Intrigue your audience, even unsettle them a bit if possible, but never insult them.

Your Monologue Should Have a Discernible Beginning, Middle, and End

This may require piecing together lines that are separated in the play text by the dialogue of other characters or by stage direction. Read your monologue for others to test it for clarity. I find it helpful to tape a reading of the monologue and listen to the piece several times to be sure the piece stands on its own.

Look for Monologues in Which Your Character Is Speaking Directly to Another Character

Monologues in which a character speaks directly to another character tend to be active and the characters' desires more readily available in performance. Monologues in which the actor speaks to the audience are also acceptable if a choice-making process is evident in the text. The danger with monologues that address the audience is that the piece will appear to be a stand-up comedy routine or a sermon, neither of which says enough about your acting ability. Ask yourself, "Will the audience know who I am, where I am, and what I'm doing?" If this answer is "absolutely not," then find yourself another monologue or consider a new edit.

Carefully Consider the Intensity Level of Your Monologue

Monologues that start at the emotional crescendo of the play are difficult to present with honesty. The audience needs more foundation, more experience with the character than you can provide in a short monologue. Also avoid monologues that remain on the same emotional plane for the duration. Even passionate monologues that show no hills and valleys are dull. Notice I said hills and valleys, not mountains and canyons. You have to take your audience with you on your brief ride. The idea is to create a very short, stand-alone, playlet.

After you have selected your monologue, spend time with the text. When producing a play, this time might be called the table talk period. For the auditionee this is your time to discuss and dialogue with your coach about the monologue. Adjudicators write time after time on the critique sheets of young actors, "I did not know to whom you were speaking." This period of analysis will solve the problem of "Who are you talking to?" Start by asking yourself the basic questions actors consider anytime they take on a role.

What Are the Given Circumstances of the Play?
In other words ask yourself, "What do I need to account for in the world of this play? What year, what country, what station in society does my character occupy, and how does this affect the choices I make?" If you are playing a character from a play by Oscar Wilde, the character will be British and as such prone to understatement and social reserve. The humor relies on the character's efforts to maintain this decorum. A character from a play by David Mamet, by contrast, will be more likely to exhibit bombast or hyperbole. The given circumstances of the play will help you determine the carriage of your character on stage, the amount of movement, even the pace of delivery.

What Is Your Character's Immediate Goal in This Monologue?
Lady Macbeth is wringing her hands and laying bare her soul with a clear goal in mind in the "out, damned spot" monologue. She wishes to rid herself of her blood-stained past. The more tangible and concrete the goal, the better. Philosophical or spiritual goals are fine and can be developed by a good actor

over the course of a full scene or play, but they are virtually impossible to breathe life into in a short audition. So even if your monologue is spiritual, psychological, or philosophical within the framework of the play, make your goals concrete. Lady Macbeth wants to get the blood off her hands. That is active and clear.

What Are the Obstacles Your Character Faces in the Monologue?

Obstacles will be the key to revealing what your character is doing. Obstacles can be other people, a physical disability, the natural world, or psychological barriers. Try to identify your obstacle very specifically. An actor performing Nora's monologue in Act Three of A *Doll's House* may decide her obstacle to leaving is a handshake. This may sound silly, but perhaps Nora simply needs to seal the separation from Torvald with a handshake, and to get the handshake, she must make him understand why she must leave. This is action with both a clear *goal*, to leave, and an *obstacle*, a handshake. Now your audience will see you at work trying to accomplish some deliberate outcome and you will be making choices in the process. When you reveal the choice-making process on stage in an engaging and interesting fashion you will have the attention and admiration of your auditors.

Identify the Relationships

The last part of the analysis puzzle you must solve is to identify the *relationships* your character has. How does your character relate to the other characters in the world of the play? Returning to Nora in Act Three of A *Doll's House*, let's look at what I mean by relationship. Nora has been married to Torvald for a number of years, they have children, and she has displayed a great deal of physical intimacy in the relationship. What we discover in her third-act monologue is that she has been emotionally and intellectually dishonest with Torvald, and now she is coming clean. This truth implies a number of emotions: regret, guilt, sadness, loneliness, anger, and resolve. Look at the great range of choices available to the actor once you have considered the truth of this relationship. Now these monologues can begin to take on added texture.

The Second Commandment—Thou Shalt Read of the Literature of the Earth, and I Say Without Ceasing

If you want a new car, the best way to know which car to buy is to go from dealer to dealer and drive as many as possible. If you are going to buy a tomato, you pick up a lot of tomatoes, squeeze them, examine them, and select the one you like. Even if you want to buy a CD, you listen to it first on the Internet to see if it is worth the price. So why is it young actors are so averse to reading plays? An actor—college, professional, or serious community theatre amateur—who takes his craft seriously should read two plays a week at a minimum and keep a running file of interesting characters and potential monologues. This is the very food that feeds your art, the written text. So read plays, lots of plays, from Indian Sanskrit drama to the most inventive contemporary work like Maria Irene Fornes and Richard Schechner. Read it all, and commit it to your working knowledge.

The choice of a monologue becomes doubly difficult when you realize how many volumes and volumes of monologue collections exist on the shelves of bookstores or on the virtual shelves of your favorite online vendor. These collected volumes do contain some wonderful monologues from some first-rate contemporary plays. But, if they are neatly packaged and made available for everyone to use, then, of course, everyone will use them. The material gets stale very quickly. The shelf life of a monologue collection book is short. Also, certain plays and playwrights become hot properties for audition material. Directors always know when Christopher Durang has penned a new play because we will see the same half-dozen monologues over and over again. Now I like Christopher Durang just fine, but a joke is only funny the first time you hear it. After that . . . well, you get the point. If you are reading plays, not collected volumes of monologues or the same tried and true authors of funny audition material, you are mining uncharted land. I remember discovering the plays of John Patrick Shanley some years before they were collected into a volume and feeling I had discovered my own personal goldmine of audition material. Maybe a new playwright is out there that you will discover, or maybe you will connect with a rich forgotten classic like Aphra Behn or Dion Boucicault. But only if you read will you uncover the unique, the untested, the fresh audition material.

Read plays with the desire to act. Look for characters in the play that you could bring to life. Find parts that can stretch your range and provide an element of risk to your work. Auditors respect risk and will often reward challenging choices. Choosing a play that may not be well known or that slid to the back of history's bookshelf presents a true challenge. Plays by the Elizabethan masters writing alongside Shakespeare provide just such fertile material. Or explore exciting new play collections such as those performed at the Humana Festival at the Actor's Theatre of Louisville. Great writers seldom go stale. O'Neill, Williams, and Miller give you a world of opportunity. However, you can also find terrific monologues in otherwise mediocre plays. So build your library, and in so doing you will build your audition portfolio.

When I say that auditors respect risk, I mean intellectual, emotional, and interpretive risk. I do not recommend playing a character outside your age range, or making a selection that requires more ability to interpret than you currently possess. If you try to perform a difficult monologue and fail, then that is an unacceptable risk. An acceptable risk is one that will shed new light on a known commodity, one that reintroduces a forgotten gem, or one that unveils previously unknown work.

Shedding new light on a known commodity means, more than anything else, making the piece an extension of your personality through interpretation. No dramatic work is better known than *Hamlet*. Several years ago I attended a performance of Hamlet at the Barbican Center in London that featured Kenneth Branagh in the title role. This stage production predated Branagh's epic filming of Shakespeare's play, and so I had no idea what to expect. What I discovered was an actor with ruthlessly sharp comic timing. I laughed out loud for large portions of the play. The new light Branagh shed for me was just how very funny this play really is. He did not misinterpret, wrongfully interpret, or sacrilegiously deface the bard's work. Instead, he added his own impish wit to the author's creation of obstacles and tensions to create a new and vibrant play out of an oft-told tale. Branagh's expression of the famous "to be or not to be" speech was hilarious as he sardonically illustrated the absurdity of the human dilemma. You are, I fear, like me, not the equal of Mr. Branagh. So you may want to steer clear of the "to be or not to be" soliloquy. But you might want to consider a lesser-known but not forgotten modern classic from *Death of a Salesman* or *The Glass Menagerie*. The auditors will certainly be familiar with any monologue you choose from either of these plays, but your fresh take may give you an edge if the auditor can see the work anew through your interpretation.

Reintroducing a forgotten gem can be an especially exciting approach to picking a monologue. I once attended a high school theatre production of Clifford Odets' *Waiting for Lefty*. Now, this play is not dead to the stage, but because the piece was written for the political climate of a particular time, it is not performed very often. This very creative high school director used a cast composed of football team members and two actresses from the school's drama program. The actresses were accomplished for their age, but the football players, well, they were raw and brutal in their honesty. Frankly I never would have believed a high school production could have done justice to that depression-era play, but I was wrong. The show had a timeless quality I could not have predicted. That high school director took a risk with a forgotten gem, and she certainly impressed me.

Introducing a previously unknown work is the trickiest of the risk-taking options. Directors with the stature to serve as auditors or casting directors tend to be well read, and abreast of the new writers on the market. The temptation for young actors seeking really fresh material is to write their own. This is, of course, fine if you happen to be Harold Pinter or David Mamet.

But the odds are that you are not. I write plays myself, but I would never trust my writing skills enough to bet my next acting role on them. I have more objectivity when I analyze the work of other writers, and can find more levels and textures. You may be a great young playwright on the verge of producing the next *Cat on a Hot Tin Roof*, but as an actor you will be wise to use the work of proven, published writers. Publishers make their living deciding what will or will not sell. Now this may sound crass and mercenary, but I trust someone whose next meal or rent depends on doing their job right. I trust publishers when they say a play has a market. Auditions are sales pitches to a much greater extent than they are art. If you do elect to go with material from an unpublished author or from an Internet source, make sure you seek a wide range of opinions on the work. If you run the monologue for a variety of actors and acting coaches, you will at least have something more than your own gut instinct to work with. One of my students recently wrote his own audition material for a large regional audition. I suspect he knew I would not approve, and so he used other coaches for his preparation. Well, you can guess the result. Now he is working with me again to prepare for the University/ Resident Theatre Association Auditions. We will use time-tested literature combined with new, not obscure, material. This time he will be ready.

The monologue you choose will be inextricably linked to your audition. Knowing this should encourage you to choose wisely from as broad a field of options as possible.

The Third Commandment— Thou Shalt Rehearse Until the Time Has Passed Away and Night Is Fallen; I Mean Rehearse a Lot

If you plan to be actually taken seriously in the audition process, you must take the process seriously. This means setting aside a time every day to work on audition material. I would recommend at least an hour. If you have a coach, work with him or her at least twice a week on your audition. Actors, like singers, must stay fresh and comfortable with the pieces they want to perform. Preparation makes for a confident, smooth auditioning experience.

I honestly believe every actor should have between fifteen and thirty working monologues in the repertoire. This suggestion goes back to our second commandment. You must read to find these monologues. Professional theatres are still impressed by those who can do justice to the great writers. Make sure your portfolio contains the works of Williams, O'Neill, Chekov, the Greek masters, and the Elizabethans. However, these writers are demanding. Preparation is essential. A Chekov monologue demands hours and hours of practice if it is to carry the rich flavor it deserves. Do not scrimp on your rehearsal time. Rehearsal is the time when you try things. You move freely, you move until you don't feel the need to pace anymore. You listen to the sound of the words and uncover the music contained in them. Rehearsal allows you to examine the places that naturally build and subsequently recede in a passage. In the rehearsal process, you can play the scene in the natural, expected fashion, then turn it on its inverse and sigh when a scream is expected or laugh when a sob seems most logical. Your coach will help you sort out what to keep and what to throw out until you finally settle into a kind of zone with the monologue that I call "full possession." The words and the experience become completely yours. Then your audience—whether they are critics, directors, or fellow students—will identify your persona totally with the persona of the monologue character. To this day there are some monologues that I associate with certain individuals; I can't separate them. I once saw a contestant in the Miss Texas Pageant (yes, that is what I said, the Miss Texas Pageant) perform Banana's monologue from *House of Blue Leaves* by John Guare. By my estimation I have seen that monologue performed eight trillion times since that Miss Texas Pageant, but that performance so stunned me, she so completely owned that play, that to this day she is Bananas in my mind. She must have spent hours and hours working and reworking, discovering and re-discovering to arrive at such utter and

11

complete ownership of that character. Guess what? If memory serves, she won the pageant.

As you rehearse, take into consideration the following basic principles of monologue staging.

Stage Your Audition with the Idea That Less Is More

Limit your activity to the essential and the compelling. How do you know what is essential? This goes back to your careful analysis of goals and obstacles. Ask yourself if the gesture or movement propels you to the goal or past the obstacle. Sometimes a simple gesture can clarify a moment when a large, overt gesture simply muddies the picture. Consider Nora again from *A Doll's House*. Nora reasons with Torvald, patiently at first, laying out for him why their marriage is a sham. The actor may wish to sit quite still in a chair as these lines are delivered, then at the moment of self-realization bolt out of the chair and take a step or two away from the spot to free Nora from Torvald's emotional grasp. This is just an example, but the idea is to make clear decisive choices on stage, linked to the goals and obstacles the character faces. Another choice would be to stand facing the audience and at the moment of discovery turn ninety degrees and take a step. The action is simple, but the mere act of separating at the right time says a great deal. Try to use a space with a radius of five to twelve feet for your audition. Anything more will seem huge and overstated. You need to rehearse your monologues in a wide variety of venues.

Not All Auditions Occur in Theatres

Theatres come in a wide range of sizes and configurations. Work monologues in small classrooms, large lecture halls, and on stages of various sizes. Large regional auditions such as the Southeastern Theatre Conference and the Southwest Theatre Association often conduct their auditions in hotel ballrooms and then host callbacks in hotel suites or rooms. The dynamics of this kind of audition are difficult to anticipate. To be mentally prepared for the adjustment, you should rehearse in awkward and distracting locales. Adjusting to performance conditions is a part of the audition. You have to develop a concentration composed of mental toughness and flexibility.

Placing Imaginary Characters Carefully

I feel very strongly that the imaginary character should never be located on stage to the direct left or right of the actor or in a chair on the stage. Locate the imaginary character downstage and slightly to the right or left of you. Find a spot on the wall above and beyond the auditors and play to that spot consistently. You do not want to work to a spot that is directly in the center of the house. If you work to downstage right or left, you can locate the character more clearly within the boundary of the fourth wall, the imaginary wall that separates actor and audience. Never look your auditors in the eye as though they are the imaginary character. This may catch their attention but it is discomforting, and they will look away from you. Avoid placing your characters upstage right or left of you for a very simple reason. Your face is your best acting feature. Show it off as much as possible. If you are talking directly to your left or right, you are giving the auditors a lot of profile. If you are standing and talking to a chair, you are also preventing the auditors from seeing your face. If you work with your face three-quarters front or straight ahead, then when you decide to turn away, the move will seem deliberate and carry maximum weight.

Many Auditors Recommend Avoiding Furniture in Your Audition

Furniture has a tendency to become the focus of the scene. One adjudicator my students auditioned for routinely dismissed any audition that used a chair or table, even though the furniture was prominently provided on the stage for the actors to use. He said his reason was that he had no interest in scenes about chairs. Virtually everyone agrees that hand props should not be employed. Hand props are regarded by auditors as gimmicks that distract from your acting skills. If your monologue demands that you acknowledge a prop like a gun, a glass, or some such object, then pantomime is appropriate. Rehearse this carefully to account for the size and weight of the object. A good pantomime moment can impress an auditor.

Remember Your Given Circumstances

Where does the scene take place? If you can successfully convey to your audience whether the scene is interior or exterior, and such factors as temperature and time of day, then you are really going to make fine marks in the auditors' book. Consider each choice you make onstage with these given circumstances in mind, then add the emotional circumstances as well. Is the surrounding familiar? Is there an element of danger? All of these considerations will add texture to your staging if you can account for them simply with a well-timed shudder, a nervous glance, or the power of a deep breath. You don't have to overdo it, but find the nonverbal action that helps you identify for the audience the world of the monologue. For example, an actor playing Abigail in Act Two, scene one of Arthur Miller's *The Crucible* should take into account that the scene occurs in a New England forest, at night, in planting season or spring. There should be a slight chill in the air for the actor and the sense of the unknown that comes with being in a forest at night. All of this should be blended with Abigail's goal of seducing John Proctor and the obstacle confronting her, the physical distance he insists they keep from each other. The actor can make a number of choices ranging from a huddled crouch on the ground to shivering with the arms folded around the torso. But as the scene unfolds, the cold and the night must seem less important than the desire and the passions. The actor's choices will change to meet the new priorities. The arms will be freer. The breathing will reflect the rising passions. Subtle recognitions of the world around you help create a believable world for you and the auditors.

The Fourth Commandment—Thou Shalt Present Thyself a Worthy Subject for Hire (It Is a Job So Act Like It)

Young actors are routinely regarded as a cliché around a university campus. Ask the average business major to describe an acting student, and you may get a phrase like, "black clothes-wearing, chain-smoking, sleepless, beret-wearing, rude freak-a-zoids." Of course this does not fairly describe them or the vast majority of university theatre students or professional actors either, but it is close enough on many counts, and for that reason I feel the need to discuss the etiquette of the audition gathering.

Have Good Manners

I once had a friend on the faculty of a university tell me, "Your best friends at this place are the custodial staff and your secretary. Treat them with respect and your life will be fine." I have tried to heed that advice to this day. At an audition your best friends are the accompanist, the runners, and the monitors operating the audition. You must never treat them rudely or with anything less than the utmost courtesy. An accompanist can either save your life onstage or choose to watch you drown. The operators running the audition deal with hundreds of egos and hundreds of glitches; your problems, glitches, and demands are neither unique nor life-threatening. My advice: smile, show everyone involved, including your fellow actors, that you are having a very good time living a life in the theatre and that part of that joy comes from being around others who love the theatre. Look, there is obvious competition. Why emphasize the point further by treating everyone in the theatre as a potential enemy? Theatre is not boxing or football; you do not gain some mental advantage by psyching out your fellow performers. All you do is alienate someone who could be a friend who, at some later date, could recommend you for a part.

Dress—This Is a Job Interview

Your wardrobe should say up front, "I am a professional." Here are some hints:

Women The most practical audition attire for a young woman is an ankle length skirts that flows (i.e., plenty of fabric of a light to medium weight) and a blouse (of similar weight) that suggests accurately your dimensions but does not flaunt too much flesh. I have seen young women make some disastrous audition choices hoping to capture the attention of a director. I have seen blouses that were too tight and that burst open at inopportune times, halters that did not halter, and perhaps most dreadful of all, miniskirts. I once heard a director at the University/Resident Theatre Association comment, "I have seen more panties today than if I had spent the afternoon at Frederick's of Hollywood." Your discomfort is our discomfort, and your mortification is our cue to look the other way and try to forget you ever auditioned. Color is important as well. Pick bright colors for your comic audition and conservative (not somber, all black is just plain grim) colors for your serious audition material. Patterned fabrics are fine if they are very subtle. Do not dress in a clown costume. You are auditioning; so you want the critics to remember your acting, not your clothes. Women can wear dark business slacks if the monologue is best suited by such a choice, but be sure your slacks fit you in a flattering fashion. Shoes are an important fashion choice as well. Women wear dance flats or character shoes. High heels, stilettos, or floppy sandals are just an invitation to disaster.

Men Please do not wear a black turtleneck. I know this may not bother most directors, but there is a large contingent of directors like me that consider this *the* cliché of the theatre. Wear a button-up sports shirt, or a dress shirt and a tie if you are comfortable in a tie and the tie fits your monologue. The colors should be conservative but not drab. Blues, tans, and reserved stripes work well. Khaki slacks are still the classic. For one thing, they fit loosely and allow you to move. They are attractive enough to pass for professional garb, and they go with everything. But a blue, loose-fitting twill will also fit the bill nicely. I would avoid a jacket unless the monologue really needs it.

For the sake of your own dignity, please do not wear jeans, a sweatshirt, or some variation of the T-shirt that sports a logo of any kind. Directors are as prone to autosuggestion as anyone else. What if the directors or critics in your auditorium harbor ill will toward Nike, Tommy Hilfiger, or the University of Michigan? I say it makes no sense to start your audition by calling attention to something other than yourself. You should also remember that casting directors and auditors are professionals and they have been away from college life for many years. What may be stylish or hip on campus can be juvenile in a job interview. Do not wear jeans, leather, Lycra, or any other fabric that calls attention to your youth and inexperience.

Shoes are an important fashion choice for men as well. Guys, the old-fashioned topsider or penny loafer are still the most perfect audition shoe styles ever designed for men. You can move freely, there is little or no heel to catch on something, and from a distance they look professional enough to pass for quality footwear.

The Fifth Commandment — You Are a Chosen People When Your Number Is Called; Take the Stage and All the Fruits That Rest Therein, at Least for the Next Ninety Seconds

If you have obeyed the first four commandments (and I know you will), you should have every reason to expect success in your audition. When your number is called, take the stage with confidence, not arrogance, and introduce yourself clearly to the house by stating your name and number. Some auditions such as URTA ask that you state the names of the plays you will be performing from. You need to know this information in advance and rehearse your introduction thoroughly. Do not spend time adjusting the furniture or turn your back to the audience to compose yourself. Just introduce yourself, do your scene, repeat your name and number, and go away.

Thou Shalt Nots of This Commandment

Thou Shalt Not Spend Time and Energy on the Furniture
Never waste your time in front of an auditor moving a chair, a table, or a stool, or using the furniture so much that the scene ceases to be about you the actor and becomes an audition for the furniture. I have suggested avoiding the use of furniture altogether if possible. If you feel furniture is essential, then for your own sake make sure you spend as little time as possible with it.

17

Thou Shalt Not Apologize   If the wheels come off, if you slop a line, go blank, or in some other way confront calamity, do not say you are sorry. You have not offended us, insulted us, or in any way inconvenienced us. You paid for this chance to audition with time and money, we invited you here, and now you are giving us your best. Sometimes things happen. Just plow on, smile, and show us your sense of humor. Then tell us your name again and proudly leave the stage.

Thou Shalt Not Speed   Be aware of your pace. The adrenalin rush of an audition can prompt even a good actor to rush a monologue. Trust the pauses and the silent moments you have found and move through the work at the pace you have rehearsed. The key here, like so much else that we have discussed, is to choose your monologue wisely. If you have a three-minute audition slot, do not feel as though you should use two minutes and fifty-nine seconds. Choose a monologue that will give a time cushion. Then you can pace the audition according to the requirements of the selection and the venue you are performing in. In a large hall you will need to enunciate very clearly, and this means you will need to slow down a bit. In a small space the relationships are more intimate, and your pace can be more natural. The monologue should have enough of a cushion to accommodate any environment. I like to allow five seconds of cushion for each minute of audition time.

2

The Tools of the Actor's Trade

Don Sandley

In every profession the artisan is expected to possess the tools to do the job. A stockbroker in the modern world needs a cell phone, a first-rate computer, and a laptop. A plumber needs . . . (oh, who am I kidding? I have no idea what the plumber calls that stuff in his truck! That's why I pay him so much to unclog my pipes). Well, actors must have the necessary tools for their trade as well. I have already mentioned the first, a good portfolio. In addition, the actor must have a professional-looking resume and a good eight-by-ten headshot.

Tool 1: The Actor's Portfolio of Audition Monologues

Include works from Elizabethan, Greek, Modernism (i.e., Shaw, Ibsen, Strindberg), and a variety of contemporary styles in your portfolio. Even if you do not fancy yourself a comic actor, have four or five comic scenes that make you look solid in that genre. College actors need twenty to thirty working monologues. High school actors would do well to have ten to fifteen.

When selecting material for your portfolio, be aware of the standard audition time frames. Auditions tend be forty-five seconds, sixty seconds, ninety seconds, two minutes, or four minutes in length. The longer audition blocks are rare and usually come into play at the callback or private audition level.

Tool 2: The Resume

Never in history has it been easier to create a professional resume. With the personal computer and the quick printing shops in every strip mall waiting to print your life story, there is no excuse for not having a first-rate resume. So I will limit my advice to content and organization. You will get all the help you need with layout by using one of the newest word processing software programs such as WordPerfect or Microsoft Word. These programs provide a template and guide you through the process step by step.

I suggest you center your name in an eye-catching but not ostentatious font, then immediately beneath include your address, phone number, e-mail address, educational background, and your agent's contact information if you have one.

You first heading should be *acting work*, starting with the most recent. Make three columns and list all of your work in the first. In column two, list the part you played, and in column three the theatre you worked for. Some directors suggest listing professional work under a separate heading apart from educational, amateur, or community theatre. I think highlighting some work as more important emphasizes your inexperience. I suggest treating all of your work as important but rotating work out of the resume as you build up experience. In other words, limit your resume to, say, the last four or five years and then select important works prior to the cutoff. This will give you a natural means of separating what should or should not be in your resume.

Your second heading should be *training*. List your dance, combat, voice, or movement training history here. Be specific. If you studied the Linklater Method, say so. If you are trained in the Alexander Technique, this may help you, so do not hide it. Certifications should be unambiguously listed here as well. If you are certified in combat, say so. If you are certified to instruct in combat, this is even better, so distinguish yourself from the pack. You do not need to repeat your university or college affiliations here if you listed them under your name.

The last category is *special skills*. Special skills obviously include oddities such as juggling, mime, magic, and other interesting performance facilities. You might also consider a brief reference here to any stagecraft skills you have acquired in your career. Nonunion houses often need people who are multitalented. If you can paint scenery, perform carpentry, or design a light plot, say so here. Do not include a special technical theatre heading on an acting resume. You are applying for an acting job, not just any job. Make sure they know you are an actor. You do not want to overlook some special skills that may make the difference at hiring time. If you are fluent in a language, say so. If you ride horses, roller skate, ice skate, or have mastered some other type of specialized sporting skill, by all means list this on the resume.

Make sure you print your resume on good-quality, professional-looking paper, or even better, the flip side of your eight-by-ten photos. Oh yeah, the eight-by-ten photos . . .

Tool 3: The Eight-by-Ten, Black-and-White Photo

The photo is the last but not least tool in your kit. Young actors are notorious for letting this one slide until too late, then paying Uncle Earl five bucks to pop off a roll of film out by the mailbox in hopes of getting something that is presentable. Spend the money and hire a talent photographer. Notice I said a *talent* photographer *not* a *talented* photographer. Many very fine portrait photographers have absolutely no idea how to shoot black-and-whites for actors. These portrait photographers want you to look perfect, or unrealistically dreamy. "Well, that's just dumb," as Ross Perot used to say. If you are too perfect, you limit the parts you maybe considered for, or even worse, when the director sees you in the flesh, you will appear to have let yourself go to pot. So what should you want in an eight-by-ten? Show your personality. Sure you want to be attractive, so dress nicely, but not formally, use a little makeup—only to cover blemishes and, for women, to accentuate the eyes and mouth a bit. Take care with the light and the background. Try to capture the real you. In other words, do not bend over backward to hide your weight,

21

Erica Nicole Curington

Height: 5'0"
Weight: 120 lbs
Eye Color: Blue-Green
Hair Color: Auburn
Vocal Range: Mezzo-Soprano

1112 Rue Maison Apt. A
Birmingham, AL 35209
(555) 123-1234

EDUCATIONAL THEATRE

Cripple of Inishmaan	Helen	Samford University Theatre
Songs for a New World	Lead Soloist	Samford University Theatre
The Children's Hour	Helen	Samford University Theatre
Guys and Dolls	Agatha	Samford University Theatre
Harvey	Veta	Samford University Theatre
The Magic Flute	Knaben 2	Samford University Theatre
Children of Eden	Mama Noah	Samford University Theatre

TECHNICAL THEATRE

Miss Alabama Pageant	Backstage Crew	Stephen Leslie Wright Center
A Flea in Her Ear	Stage Manager	Samford University Theatre
The Children's Hour	Properties	Samford University Theatre
Guys and Dolls	Scenery	Samford University Theatre

DIRECTORIAL

Death Knocks	Director	Samford University Theatre
"Between the Lines"	Co-Director	Samford University Theatre
		Samford University Musical Theatre Ensemble

TELEVISION
Ivan Leonard Chevrolet commercial series

DIALECTS
Irish
British

Figure 2–1.

Figure 2–2.

your crooked nose, or any other slight distinguishing feature. That big chin might be exactly what the director is looking for. It certainly has not hurt Jay Leno. Have the photographer shoot a number of shots against a variety of backgrounds and from several angles. Then take the proofs to a handful of people you trust, especially to directors, and ask for their opinion. You will have absolutely no objectivity about your own photos. Let these trusted colleagues select one and go for it.

I have included sample resumes and headshots that I feel display what I am recommending.

23

Kelly Dawn Miller

Address: 1112 Rue Maison Apt. A
Homewood, AL 35206
Phone: (555) 123-1234

Vocal Range: Alto II to Soprano I
Hair Color: Brown (will dye or cut)
Eye Color: Blue
Height: 5'4"
Weight: 110 lbs

Professional Theatre Experience:

Trumpet in the Land	Esther/Indian	Trumpet in the Land (OOHDA)
The White Savage	Katherine	Trumpet in the Land (OOHDA)

Regional Theatre Experience:

The Crucible	Betty	Kurofune Theatre Co.

Educational Theatre Experience:

Snoopy	Sally	Samford University
Betrayal	Emma	Samford University
The Children's Hour	Catherine	Samford University
Guys and Dolls	Adelaide	Samford University
Children of Eden	Yonah	Samford University
The Passion	Angel	Samford University
Kindertransport	Eva	Samford University
The Crucible	Abigail	Christian Academy in Japan
Fiddler on the Roof	Hodel	Christian Academy in Japan

Directing/Assistant Directing Experience:

The Red Coat	Director	Samford University
Floyd Collins	Asst. Director	Samford University
Flea in Her Ear	Asst. Director	Samford University
Harvey	Asst. Director	Samford University

Technical Experience:

Phantom of the Opera	Dresser	Alabama City Stages (Broadway Tour)
Riders to the Sea	Stage Management	Samford University
Art	Sound Crew	Samford University
Children of Eden	Set Construction	Samford University
Translations	Properties	Samford University
Keely and Du	Publicity	Samford University

Educational/Training:
B.A. degree in theatre from Samford University (May 2001)
Four years vocal training (Martha Tarter, Dr. Randall Richardson)
Dance/movement training: Killian Manning

Special Talents: Directable, adaptable, moves well, strong stage presence, dialects (German, English, Irish, Southern, and more), plays piano/reads music, rides horses, swims, skis, drives a stick shift

Figure 2–3.

Figure 2–4.

Once your toolbox is complete, you are ready to audition. Audition opportunities spring up all the time. There are, however, a few large auditions that cater to those just starting out in their professional career. I have included a partial list of those I am most familiar with. Some of these organizations have websites now that can help you register online and provide you with the specific requirements for their audition. Consider your material carefully. Explore the suggestions we make in the next chapter, and break a leg!

3

What Musical Directors Look For—The Writ of Musical Theatre

Randall Richardson

A number of years ago I auditioned for *Fiddler on the Roof* hoping to be chosen for the role of Motel, the tailor. I assumed that since my classical voice training had prepared me to sing high notes, and since I usually received good reviews on my acting in operas, I could act the part of the timid tailor. After the audition, the director (who had directed me in an opera the season before) pulled me aside and told me that my character type and voice were just too strong to portray Motel. I was finally cast as the Russian who sings during the tavern scene. All those years I had prepared to look and sing like a romantic tenor lead had backfired. I had forgotten the old saying "Beware of what you wish for, because you may get it." This experience taught me a valuable lesson. Like Don, I learned that when auditioning for musical theatre I should tailor my audition material to fit my personal inventory of abilities.

Selecting and Preparing the Song

In musical theatre auditions you need to sing a song well, so you need to choose the right song for your type of appearance and temperament. This makes the job of selecting audition music difficult. Students who need music for an upcoming audition often approach me for help. When questioned about the date of the audition, they usually give a date that is ridiculously close. In such cases, my options to help them are limited. For starters, voices are so different that familiarity with a singer is required to pick songs that show off the best part of the voice. When you start early you'll have much more time to pick the right song by answering questions about yourself like the following: What's your vocal range and the weight of your voice (heavy, light, dark, bright, etc.)? Are you a good musician? Can you sustain high or low ranges for extended periods of time? Do you have the ability to sing long phrases? Can you belt and if so, how high? How are you usually typecast?

In Chapter 1 Don listed commandments for the actor's audition process. I offer proverbs (or words of wisdom) that will help bring you success in your musical audition. **Proverb 1**: *Early preparation is most often the difference between success and failure.* During the fall semester our actors prepare for a ninety-second audition that will lead to a regional audition for summer acting/singing jobs. Two months before the auditions I began reminding my students to choose a monologue, so that I could help them pick a song excerpt that would complement it. I picked out song excerpts for ten of my students, but only three ended up singing in their auditions. One or two of the students had legitimate excuses, but the others just didn't prepare early enough to have the confidence to sing. Two of the students who began their preparations early broke to the regional level, but at least two more (who were equally talented) could have if they had sung. As a teacher, I see more students who fail because they haven't prepared than because of lack of talent.

If Choosing Audition Music Is So Complicated, Why Sing?

Proverb 2: *If you can carry a tune—sing.* If I were a young actor, I would take all the voice lessons I could afford. The performance field is narrow, and the available jobs go to the cream of the crop, so if you can sing well your chance of being hired is greatly increased. Singing not only qualifies you for more jobs (two fields—singing and nonsinging), but you also have a distinct advantage over actors who have had no vocal training. Even if you don't have a great voice, take heart. The history of musical theatre is full of stars with minimal singing voices. The names Rex Harrison, Nathan Lane, Marlon Brando, and Carol Channing come instantly to mind.

In my experience, I have found very few people who are tone deaf (or as we say today—pitch challenged). Most people have trouble singing in tune because of technical problems (how they sing). They "think" the correct pitch, but the physical act of singing prevents them from singing the right pitch. A good voice teacher and hard work can usually help anyone overcome pitch problems, so don't let this keep you from singing in auditions. I have a student from the community who came to me two years ago with no musical background. In our first lesson I discovered very quickly that she couldn't match a pitch when I played it on the piano. I enjoy a challenge, and she was a delight to teach because she worked hard and loved singing. After two years of hard work, she's made tremendous improvement and sings perfectly in tune when her melody is played with the accompaniment. I'm confident that one day she will be able to sing well without her melody being played and will be ready to perform in community theatre.

Where Do You Go for Help?

Selecting appropriate audition music is often difficult for actors because you've devoted most of your training to the spoken word rather than the sung word. For this reason, it's usually a good idea to get help in the selection of music. We singers are too close to our voices to objectively critique those songs that we sing. Using a tape recorder for feedback helps, but it can't answer questions or make suggestions like a teacher.

A number of people can help in selecting music for auditions, but the first person you should go to is a voice teacher who's familiar with the demands of musical theatre and who enjoys teaching musical theatre performers. Not all voice teachers are agreeable to working with musical theatre performers because most teachers have been classically trained, and the nonclassical singing style often demanded by musical theatre makes them uncomfortable. Nevertheless, a sympathetic voice teacher will not only be able to help you select music appropriate for your voice but can also help you sing the song better. The first place to contact is your local university. Most colleges and universities employ voice teachers for the music majors and one of these teachers might give lessons to people who are outside of the university.

Theatre directors and theatre music directors are also good resources for choosing repertoire. They will probably have had extensive experience in musical theatre auditions, and they can direct you to music that you can work on by yourself or take to a voice teacher. Many of the musical excerpts in this book were first heard in theatre auditions. If you live in a city that supports a large number of musical theatre productions (New York, for example), there are many people who make their living as musical theatre coaches. They play for auditions and give lessons. Many will have a library of musical theatre music or will be able to give you names of possible audition songs. If a coach is not available, look for a local pianist who has experience playing for musical productions. At the very least, a good pianist who can play through your music and offer objective opinions on possible audition material will be helpful. **Proverb 3**: *Face the facts. Private lessons, coaching, or hiring a pianist will cost money, but don't look at it as an expense, look at it as an investment in your career.*

Picking a Song Is Like Picking a Monologue — You've Got to Be Honest

Polonius is a doddering fool in *Hamlet*, but he gives one good piece of advice for the would-be auditioner, "To thine own self be true." As you select music, you need to be aware of the type of character you will project when you audition. Both Don and I have related our experiences with typecasting, so I won't revisit the subject except to repeat that it's important to pick music that corresponds to your personality, body type, and voice. If you're a young, slim, pert, attractive woman with a beautiful lyric soprano voice you should sing Laurie's songs "Many a New Day" or "Out of My Dreams" from *Oklahoma!* rather than Rose's "Everything's Coming up Roses" from *Gypsy*. Go with your strengths.

When you select your audition music, it will be helpful if you ask a friend or friends to give you objective opinions about your performance of it. Any opinion is better than none, and sometimes the layman will notice things that we "professionals" do not. If you ask friends for a critique, don't forget to remind them to be brutally honest. In a voice seminar I once asked my students to critique each other in writing. One young man wrote "nice dress" as a critique of a female friend's performance. Understandably, he didn't want to hurt her feelings, but he did her more harm by not giving any constructive criticism. It will be difficult for friends to be critical, but that's exactly what you need to perfect your audition material. **Proverb 4**: *The truth often hurts, but it can get you work.*

Preparation Is Your Key to Success

Proverb 5: *A music audition isn't the lottery.* You can't pick five numbers or scratch the surface and hope to win. What you must have is a box full of tools that will equip you to handle any situation that you're given. In addition to voice lessons, you should also consider piano lessons. Auditions are stressful for everyone but if an audition involves singing, and you don't read music, it can be *really* intimidating. The musical skills you acquire from piano lessons will enable you to learn music on your own and to explain clearly to the audition pianist how your music is to be played. In addition, these musical skills will prepare you to adjust to unexpected changes in the audition with more confidence. A few years ago I observed a young woman's voice lesson in New York that occurred immediately after she had auditioned for a show. She tearfully told her teacher that she had prepared to sing her audition songs, but when she arrived at the audition, she was asked to sight-read music from the show. She was understandably upset about having to sing unfamiliar music in the audition, but what she didn't realize was that if she had sight-read well, she might have gotten the role simply because of her musical ability. No director wants to worry about actors who have trouble learning their music. A "quick study" has a definite advantage over a performer who learns slowly. My ability to learn music quickly has gotten me a number of "last-minute" jobs over the years.

Other musical tools that you might consider keeping in your toolbox include membership in a band or choir. If you've had experience in either type of ensemble, you should continue participation and note this in your bio. Don related a story to me about an audition he once held for a production of *Godspell*. When casting came down to two young women of equal talents, the one who had listed her experience playing the recorder was hired because he thought it would be unique to let her play a tune while on stage. So keep practicing that flügelhorn—it might get you a job someday.

One of the most useful tools an actor in musical theatre can have is dance experience. I have regretted many times my lack of dance training, and you will too if you can't dance. When I lived in Kansas City my first love was opera, but one year I decided that I wanted to try my luck at musical theatre. A female friend of mine was also interested in musical theatre, so we went to a summer theatre open audition that was attended by a large number of companies. After we sang, we received several callbacks and decided that we liked Music Theatre of Wichita the best, so we told the music director we'd return when they had their next round of auditions. I could tell that he'd liked my singing because he gave me the script that I would read and suggested the song that I should sing. Several weeks later, we returned to the audition. I was wearing my three-piece suit (customary attire for the opera auditions I had been singing) and my friend was wearing a blouse, long skirt, and boots. We felt pretty good about our reading and singing audition, but I knew I was in trouble when they asked us to go down the hall to the dance audition. I knew I was in *big* trouble when we walked into the room and everyone else had on leotards and tights. Needless to say, the twenty measures of modern dance that I performed in the audition wasn't exactly the dance that the choreographer had taught us minutes before. As I think back on that audition, I'm grateful that the video camera had not been invented yet. I might have seen myself on *America's Funniest Home Videos* at a later date.

If you're a great actor and dancer but have limited singing and musical skills, don't give up hope. When I first thought of writing a book like this, I was thinking of my theatre major voice students who were not taking any other music courses and who often needed help in selecting audition music because they couldn't read music.

Don't Get Caught Off Guard

I've attended many auditions and one thing always amazes me. Many of the actors would have done better if their preparation have been more thorough. All the voice lessons in the world will not help if you enter an audition without serious preparation of your audition materials, knowledge of performance conditions, and proper warm-up habits. If you heed the following proverbs you'll enter most auditions a few steps ahead of most of your competition.

Proverb 6: *Pick the right music for your voice and character type.* When you sing in an audition you want to sing your very best, so bear in mind that some songs will sound better in your voice than others. It is tempting to choose an outstanding song you've heard someone else sing well, but if the song doesn't "fit" your voice, it won't help your audition. The song you sing should be one that you sing well on both good and bad days. It's always better to sing an easy song well than to sing a difficult song badly.

Proverb 7: *Find out as much as you can about the audition in advance.* Some questions to ask are: What show/shows are you auditioning for? How large is the room? Who is the pianist (in other words, how well does the pianist sight-read)? How much time will you have with the pianist? Will there be warm-up rooms available? What's the time limit for auditions? This information should be available from the people organizing the audition; however, if you still have questions you should ask acquaintances who've participated in the auditions before. The fewer surprises you have, the more relaxed you'll be and the better you'll perform.

Proverb 8: *Choosing your song and monologue requires some thought.* Make sure that they either blend together or that they have a sharp contrast and show your range (both vocally and dramatically). If you've ever attended an all-day audition you know that after a few hundred performances the judges are numb, so if you draw a high number you better be outstanding or you'll be forgotten. On the last day of a Southeastern Theatre Conference regional audition I once attended, we were all punch-drunk until an African American actor delivered a monologue about being tired of being cast in all the servant roles, calling the boss "massah," and singing about the Mississippi River. He vowed to never accept this type of role again. He was good, but we had heard a lot of good actors in the eight hundred who had gone before him. However, he got everyone's attention, laughter, and a standing ovation when he sang "Old Man River." He probably got a lot of job offers because of his originality.

Proverb 9: *Choose audition material that will allow you to end your audition with a few seconds to spare.* You make a better impression when you finish intentionally rather than by having time called on you. Most of the theatre directors you audition for won't need an extra four or five seconds to evaluate you. They know exactly what they're looking for and have made a decision long before your time is exhausted. Last year, a theatre major at our school went to an audition and according to her score would have broken to the regional audition if she hadn't gone over her ninety-second time limit. The story is even more tragic because she went over as a result of the pianist playing her song extremely slowly. She could have prevented this problem by focusing her preparation in a number of areas. First, she should have prepared her monologue so thoroughly that she could vary the tempo and pacing to compensate for lost time in the song. Second, she probably didn't have a definite tempo in mind for her song and wasn't able to clearly communicate the tempo to the pianist. I try to prepare my theatre students for auditions by making them explain to their pianist the tempo they want to sing. Many of them have never set the tempo themselves and have just relied on the pianist to lead them. However, after a few bad performances at wrong tempos, the students begin to think about the correct tempo before they instruct the pianist. In my experience, many theatre students have not had a musical background and usually feel uncomfortable setting tempos for pianists. All I can say is—you are in charge of setting the tempo, not the pianist! When your time comes to give instructions to the pianist, you should very quietly sing (assuming that someone else is auditioning while you're with the pianist) the first few phrases for him so that he will get a feel for how you'll perform the song. Finally, if the pianist plays too fast or too slow, you should lead him to the correct tempo. This is why they call him an accompanist.

The best ways to lead a pianist to a new tempo is to *gradually* push the tempo (and pianist) faster or slower. You must do this gradually, because if you do it quickly your pianist will be suddenly ahead or behind you. It might take you two lines of music to find the correct tempo but it will be worth the effort. Not only will you have a better chance at finishing within your allotted audition time, but you will also show your judges that you are an accomplished performer who doesn't get rattled when things go awry.

Proverb 10*: If an audition calls for sixteen measures of music it's usually possible to sing more.* A sixteen-measure stipulation assumes that the excerpt will be in four-four time (around thirty seconds). If you have a great up-beat excerpt in two-four or three-four time you can sing more measures in the same amount of time that four-four time would have taken because of the fewer beats in each measure. Just make sure that the extra measures are necessary and enhance your performance.

Proverb 11: *When choosing music, look for songs that are not overdone.* The singing audition should center on the talents of the singer and the song choice should not be part of the judging; however, after hearing the same song many times, judges begin to tune it out. If you perform an overly familiar song well, by all means sing it, but if you perform other unique songs equally well, it might be wise to choose one of those. As with monologues, songs go in and out of fashion and you should keep abreast of the songs that are performed too much. As a small investor I learned a valuable lesson in the early 1980s. I bought some gold as an investment during the summer, and within a few months it had doubled in price. By fall, inflation was high and every night the news stations would show footage of people standing in line to buy gold. The lesson learned by most of those who bought gold at this time was that if you invest in what is in vogue you're too late. Many of the latecomers lost money when the price of gold went down. The only ones to make money were the ones who bought gold before it was popular to do so. I tell this story to emphasize the fact that if you choose to perform the popular song of the day, everyone else will probably have the same idea and that great song will loose its uniqueness because of overuse. Choose less performed songs of quality rather than popular ones that everyone sings.

Proverb 12: *Look for song excerpts that demonstrate a variety of emotions.* Picking a song is like picking a monologue—it must go somewhere. You should take your judges on a journey even if it's only a sixteen-bar one. Locating excerpts that display contrasting moods is difficult because audition time is usually limited, and most excerpts are so short they display only one emotion. In spite of this, the following suggestions might help you to "jazz up" your song excerpt:

- Choose music immediately preceding the climax or ending of a song because it is often in a different mood.
- As long as the key is the same and the transition is not too drastic, musical material from different parts of a song can be combined.
- Music from different songs can be spliced together when they are in the same key. This can produce an interesting audition excerpt and is the reason I include song excerpt keys in the catalogue.

Proverb 13: *If possible, investigate the abilities of the audition pianist.* If the pianist is very good and is acquainted with musical theatre song literature, you can put most songs in front of her and be happy with the accompaniment; however, if the pianist's abilities are unknown, you should choose songs that require less coordination and practice between singer and pianist. Music that's unfamiliar to the pianist might result in tempo and harmonic surprises, and you will be the one to suffer. Furthermore, never assume that the pianist will be able to transpose your music or read a chord chart. Provide her with written-out music in the correct key.

You should also make your music both question and accident proof. You'll probably have a limited amount of time to instruct the pianist, so make sure that your music is easy to read and clearly marked. When using photocopies, make certain that the accompaniment is not cut off on the top, bottom, or sides, and mark important moments (holding notes, slowing down, speeding up, etc.) in the excerpt with a highlighter. It is also helpful to cut and paste your music so that the pianist has only the music that you'll perform in front of him. If he has to jump from a measure on one page to a measure on another page, there could be problems. Music should also be placed in a notebook or mounted on cardboard so that it doesn't blow off the piano while you're singing.

Proverb 14: *As you prepare a song, invest in time with your own pianist and become extremely familiar with your music.* It is often helpful to rehearse with your pianist in different rooms and

37

halls in order to grow accustomed to adjusting your singing and hearing to larger or smaller spaces. No matter how quietly the piano is played, you want to be able to sing in the correct key by listening and tuning to what you hear.

In your preparations, you should remember that singing is a physical endeavor. You are no different from the athlete who runs a two-hundred-meter race; the athlete and the singer use muscles in the body. Just as the athlete must adopt a daily regimen of running, you should adopt a daily regimen of practice. There is an old saying, "If you skip practice one day, you can tell; if you skip practice two days, your voice teacher can tell; if you skip practice three days, the whole world can tell."

One of my students, who was Miss Alabama a few years ago, sang a rather difficult arrangement in the Miss America Pageant. Two months before the pageant I gave her four to five voice lessons each week (on a two-minute song!) so that every part of the song would be "grooved" into her voice. This is similar to the way a professional tennis player "grooves" his swing to be the same every time he swings. Our hard work paid off. In spite of hoarseness caused by too many performances a few weeks before the pageant, she still sang well. Her voice was so accustomed to singing the song correctly that it took over for her in performance. She placed third runner-up and was the crowd favorite to win. When you're in front of the judges for only ninety seconds you want to be extremely prepared, so you can perform your best under all circumstances.

Proverb 15: *If you must provide your own pianist or use taped accompaniment, choose the pianist.* Although most auditions provide a pianist, some may not, so you should always be ready to bring your own. Paying a pianist is more expensive, but a pianist will enable you to perform more expressively because you'll be free to vary the tempo. A piano will also sound better than accompaniment played by a tape player. If you're not given the option of being accompanied by a piano, you should ask if taped accompaniment or *a cappella* singing is preferred. Both have advantages and disadvantages. Taped accompaniment gives you an accompaniment to sing with, but it limits your spontaneous expression and carries the possibility of being too loud or too soft. There's also the danger that the tape machine might "eat" your tape in the middle of the audition. A *cappella* singing gives you complete freedom of expression and the opportunity to pick a key that fits your voice best in the event that you are a little under the weather. However, if your judges are accustomed to hearing accompaniment (as most are), your performance might sound rather stark. Before singing *a cappella* in an audition, you also need to be very secure singing without accompaniment so that you don't change the key.

Proverb 16: *When your audition requires a monologue and a song—sing first.* If you speak first, you put yourself at risk for the following reasons:

- When there are large numbers of people auditioning, your time with the pianist will be very short (probably a few moments before you go on stage). If you perform your monologue first, the pianist will usually confer with the next actor while you deliver your monologue. This sequence of events will put another song accompaniment in the pianist's thoughts, moments before he plays your accompaniment.
- Actors often perform a monologue and become so involved in the emotion of the monologue that they are unable to switch to singing mode. Sometimes this causes an actor to sing the wrong opening notes or out of tune. I've seen actors sing entire excerpts in the wrong key because they were unable to make the transition from monologue to song.
- If you're performing a vocally taxing, dramatic monologue it will probably affect your voice adversely. Singing is very difficult after performing a monologue that requires shouting, screaming, or yelling.

After giving the reasons for singing first in an audition, I am reminded that I occasionally suggest to students that they sing after a monologue. Although I never suggest the reversal to a weak musician, I sometimes recommend it when I find a great song excerpt that will get the judge's attention if it's sung after the monologue. In this situation, the probability of grabbing the judge's attention outweighs the possibility of not singing quite as well. Recently, a student approached me about finding a song excerpt for a monologue from *The Miss Firecracker Contest* by Beth Henley. The monologue was Popeye's explanation about how she got her name. Her brother threw some gravel in her eyes and then gave her some drops (ear drops) to help them. After that, she had to wear glasses, and her eyes puffed out. I drew a blank as I searched for songs to complement the monologue but I knew I'd struck gold when I remembered a song from Dan Goggin's *Balancing Act*. The title of the song was "Let's Get More Men into Nursing." You can imagine how heartbroken I was when the student backed out of the audition (lack of preparation strikes again). I can still imagine the laughter of the judges—they will never know what they missed!

Proverb 17: *On the day of the audition you should warm up and practice at home (or in your hotel room) before leaving for the audition.* When there are large numbers of people auditioning, you will not have much time in a warm-up room. Actors are usually given one big room for warm-up, and vocalizing in a room full of other people doing the same thing is difficult. An earlier warm-up will enable you to shorten your warm-up time at the audition and will assure you of being prepared vocally when it's time for your audition.

As you begin your warm-up you should start with some type of aerobic exercise. Aerobic exercise warms your body by pumping blood faster and requiring deeper breaths. This type of exercise helps the body to function as if it were much later in the day, even if it is early in the morning. Avoid strenuous exercise however, especially if you're unaccustomed to it. You don't want to exhaust yourself before the audition.

Proverb 18: *Who wants to be Miss Congeniality? You do!* Whenever I go to beauty pageants and a Miss Congeniality award is given, I always assume that it's basically a consolation prize for a nice girl who isn't good enough to win. In fact, as a young man in college I often heard my fraternity brothers refer to Miss Congeniality whenever they talked about a girl who was less than pretty. Being congenial in an audition setting is much more important, however, because it can lead to landing that acting job you want. Even though Don mentioned good audition manners in Chapter 1, I would also like to give my opinion on their importance to the aspiring actor.

Since you're reading this book, you've probably already been to some auditions and have been around other actors like yourself. You've also found that some of the other actors are "class acts," the type of people you'd like to know better. However, some of the actors are the opposite, and you can't wait to get away from them. Try to be the type of person that other people want to spend more time with, especially all those people who run the auditions and the theatre directors who are hiring. A director once said to me that he was looking for actors he'd like to spend the summer with. He'd learned a long time before that if the actors he hired were difficult to work with, the summer wouldn't be very enjoyable. I've seen an example of how a bad attitude can affect a career firsthand. A singer who studied at my school a number of years ago had considerable success early in her career; unfortunately, her egotistical behavior cost her a number of jobs, and her career took a nosedive. It's hard to be even-tempered when you're under the pressure of an audition and things go wrong, but it will be to your advantage if you learn to handle problems positively, and treat those running the audition graciously. The lady at the sign-in desk that can't find your registration materials might be doing the hiring in your next audition. Be a nice guy, it doesn't cost you anything.

Proverb 19: *Arrive early—stay late*. If you arrive at the audition site early you can familiarize yourself with the space, meet key people, and settle into your surroundings. If you arrive late, you'll probably be flustered and short on concentration, and you may miss the audition entirely. A student I know has the skills and resume to be a prime candidate for a first-class M.F.A. program. In his senior year he scheduled a graduate school audition but left home late, allowing himself almost no window of time for unexpected disasters as he made the three-hour trip. He arrived at the audition site, couldn't find a parking place, and wound up missing his audition by thirty minutes. Needless to say, he didn't get accepted.

Proverb 20: *Stay performance healthy and drink—water.* Most people walk around in a state of dehydration every day because it's not noticeable to the average person; however, when you sing hydration is extremely important. If you're dehydrated, the mucus around your vocal cords thickens and necessitates throat clearing at inopportune times— perhaps when you're going for that high note at the end of your song. I once read a study that concluded that if an average-sized adult were to lie in bed for twenty-four hours, it would take about 2½ litres of water to replace the liquid that the body had lost. Imagine the amount of liquid your body needs during a day of acting, singing, and dancing auditions. The best method for checking hydration is to observe your urine. If your urine is clear, you're hydrated. Remember—"pee-pale."

Sleep is also very important to the singer, and my experience with young singers and actors is that they often don't get enough sleep the night before an audition. The previous analogy of a singer being an athlete should also be considered when you choose your sleep habits. An athlete will make sure that he sleeps well the night before a big race, and a singer should get plenty of sleep before an audition. Because of our active lifestyles, the effect of sleeplessness is being studied quite a bit by scientists today. I have seen two informative documentaries on sleep. One concluded that lack of sleep often caused the same symptoms as having too much to drink. Another theorized that the high number of "friendly-fire" victims suffered by the United States during the Gulf War was in part caused by soldiers who were sleep deprived. When you operate on less than optimum sleep, your brain activity slows. This is not a good option for a singer, who must think of a number of things simultaneously: words, notes, rhythms, entrances, expression, dynamics, and the monologue that follows. The brain is a remarkable computer, but it can only handle so much input and output if it's tired. Lack of sleep also adversely affects the singer's voice. If the body is tired, the voice will also be tired and will lack stamina.

While I am preaching, I would like to warn you about drinking alcohol and smoking. Both of these drugs can greatly hurt your chances of a good audition. Let's suppose you've driven all day and upon arriving at the hotel meet some of your friends. They suggest a visit to the popular bar in town to unwind, and since your audition isn't until tomorrow afternoon you decide to go. After a few drinks everyone is having a great time and the noise level gets higher and higher. You light up a cigarette and enjoy smoking, drinking, speaking, and laughing very loudly for several hours until the party breaks up. At this point you've probably blown your chances for singing well the next day. All the alcohol you drank will dehydrate you and cause mucus around your vocal cords to become much thicker, resulting in throat clearing and perhaps coughing. The cigarette smoke you inhaled probably irritated your vocal cords and could cause excessive fluid build up in your larynx. Let's suppose you were lucky, and the alcohol and cigarette smoke had no physical effect on you. Unfortunately, you've still blown it. The hours of talking and laughing at a much louder level than normal probably exhausted your voice, which would be very noticeable in your singing audition. Be smart—celebrate after the audition.

Proverb 21: *Spend as much time as possible with the audition pianist.* At most auditions there's a "hedge" of some type that prevents one actor from monopolizing the pianist's time, but don't be shy. The pianist can help or hurt your audition, and you want to spend as much time with her as possible. I once attended a large audition organized to give actors an opportunity to speak to the pianist during monologues and was amazed to see that many times the chair next to the pianist remained empty while monologue after monologue was presented. Once again, don't be shy!

Proverb 22: *Ask the pianist to play the first three or four notes of your song as an introduction.* The pressure of the audition often causes some actors to forget the song's melody and key when only one note is given. Hearing a few notes of the opening melody as an introduction will give you a much better idea of what comes next. If the actors I referred to in Proverb 16 had requested the first few notes as an introduction, they might not have sung their entire excerpt in a different key.

Proverb 23: *If you have a bad start in your song (no matter whose fault) and can't get back on track, don't apologize, just stop and tell the pianist to start again.* You should mark a "start-over" location (nearer to the end) in your music in case there are problems. Sometimes recovering from a musical problem will work in your favor. A smooth recovery will show that you knew there was a problem and that you had the confidence to take control of the situation. If I were casting, I would want to hire someone with a clear head who knew how to get back on track when her "train" had derailed.

Proverb 24: *Don't be too theatrical.* Save your movement for the monologue. The judge might have his head down writing and listening while you're doing those great cartwheels as you sing. Interpret your song well, but don't get too complicated.

Proverb 25: *Remember the little things that say, "I'm a pro."* Say your name at the beginning and end of your performance, be crystal clear on where to enter and where to exit, and don't rely on props. In one audition I attended, the actors entered through a door that was upstage right. The door was painted black and the stage was surrounded by a black curtain. In one day I saw three or four actors who couldn't remember the location of the door after their audition. As they hunted for the door by moving the curtain, the judges yelled directions to the exit. Do you want to make that kind of impression on the judges? In other auditions I've seen performers forget their music on the piano and have to return for it, or leave in such a hurry that their feet slip out from under them. Think about it! This type of behavior doesn't make a good first impression, and in open auditions first impressions are extremely important. If you were auditioning these actors, would you hire someone who was forgetful or who had a bad sense of direction on stage when they were under pressure? They might do something similar in a production. Be aware of everything around you, from the beginning of the audition to the end. It's difficult to "keep your head" when you're filled with audition anxiety, but you can do it.

Proverb 26: *Be prepared for callback auditions and interviews.* Don spoke about the portfolio you need for callbacks in an acting audition. You also need a portfolio of songs in contrasting styles (upbeat, ballad, lyrical, belt, 50s, 60s, rock, swing, etc.) for a singing callback. As I prepare students for the type of audition that has callbacks, I always (well— almost always) remind them to be prepared for any kind of song request during the callback. A few years ago I must have forgotten to stress the importance of this type of preparation to one of my freshmen. As we worked on her semester repertoire, I chose songs that were different in style for callbacks. After the initial audition she received quite a few callbacks, but she didn't think about taking her extra music when she went to meet the interested companies. In one callback she was asked to sing a song that contrasted her original audition song, but she didn't have any other music with her. Instead, they asked her to sing "Happy Birthday" *a cappella*. The next time she auditions, I suspect she'll take additional music with her. Whenever auditions are held in large convention centers, pianos are scarce, so you might need to sing *a cappella* in your callbacks. This is very probable if callbacks are held in a hotel room. As you prepare for this situation, the best investment you'll make will be a pitch pipe (found in most music stores). Not only will you be able to sing in any key you want, but having a pitch pipe will make you appear to be more professional.

Proverb 27: *If you're sick—don't call a friend.* A few years ago, I had a student who came to me and complained that he'd been dancing at a party and had experienced shortness of breath, dizziness, and a rapid heartbeat. As we talked, I discovered that he'd previously experienced sinus problems and a well-meaning friend had given him two different pills to take. Unfortunately, the friend didn't know the ingredients of the two pills. Both pills contained the same decongestant, and by taking two pills my student doubled the dosage. At about the same time period, a few high school basketball players in our area were taking the same decongestant (also found in diet pills and recently taken off the market) to enhance their performance. Unfortunately, one of them died during a game as a result of side effects from the medication. My student was very lucky. If he had continued his strenuous dancing he might have met the same fate as the basketball player.

As a voice teacher, I am constantly around students with sinus problems, coughs, allergy problems, hoarseness and laryngitis, upper respiratory infections, and so on, so hereafter, when I refer to sickness, I'm referring to the types of illness that usually interfere with singing. If you're like most people, you don't know much about the different ingredients that medicines contain, so you should always seek help from someone who does. If I have a sick student who doesn't have any singing commitments or auditions in the near future, I usually suggest that they see a pharmacist, describe their symptoms, and ask about the best over-the-counter medicine (in some states pharmacists can prescribe certain prescription medicines) for their symptoms. A pharmacist knows the ingredients of the medications, what those ingredients will do for your symptoms, and the best over-the-counter medicine on the market. Furthermore, when I question my sick students about their medication they often say that they're taking a medicine that advertises extensively and everyone knows about it. Often, this medicine is not the best one for their symptoms. The best medicine is perhaps unknown to you but one that your pharmacist can recommend.

If my student is ill and has a singing commitment in the near future, I usually suggest that he see a doctor. This is especially important if the student is experiencing hoarseness or laryngitis. The convenience of the popular drop-in doctors' clinics (or "doc-in-the-box" as my allergist calls them) makes it much easier for performers to get immediate help (especially on weekends). However, if a student has an important commitment and appears to need a specialist, I recommend that she see an ear, nose, and throat doctor (ENT) who is sympathetic to singers. A sympathetic doctor is important because if you need to sing "tomorrow" you need a doctor who will get you through "tomorrow's" concert or audition. An unsympathetic doctor might treat you in a way that will get you through a concert or audition "next week." Both doctors could be good ones, but one might understand the necessity of a scheduled performance or audition better than the other. If you don't have a list of local ENTs who treat singers and actors you should make one now. Also, if you get sick while you are at an audition (especially one lasting several days) you should talk to the other actors from the area or to the person who's coordinating the event. Someone will probably know of a good ENT in the area.

Before I wear out the subject, let me give one more word of advice. If you feel that you're getting sick, get help immediately. In my experience, students tend to wait until they've been sick for a number of days and the audition is close before they decide to see a doctor. By that time it's often too late for modern medicine to help them in time for the audition. Singers should always follow the old adage "An ounce of prevention is worth a pound of cure."

Proverb 28: *You should have nerves of steel—not jelly.* We all get nervous when we perform, and some of us get more nervous than others whenever we sing. It's rather nerve-racking when we do something that we aren't completely confident about. Most actors and singers have their own ways to deal with the stress of a performance, so I won't go into a lengthy discussion of what to do when you're nervous; however, I'd like to mention two resources that deal with enhancing performance. First, Timothy Gallwey's books (*The Inner Game of Music, The Inner Game of Tennis,* and others) should be read by anyone who performs. When I read about his ideas on performance the first time, I realized immediately that he had perfectly analyzed my thinking when I sang or played tennis. His concepts are applicable to any type of performance. My other suggestion is that you mentally visualize your future performance in advance of the actual event. Not long ago I read an excellent article in *Newsweek* (September 25, 2000) about athletes training for the Olympics in Australia. According to the article, many of the athletes mentally visualized their perfect performance as part of their training. Scientists are just beginning to understand the power that the brain has over the body. In one study, a group of volunteers imagined tensing and relaxing one of their fingers for four weeks. At the end of the experiment, the strength in their fingers had increased by 20 percent. In another study, a group of people who mentally practiced a five-finger piano exercise improved their playing without touching the keyboard. Perhaps recognition of this phenomenon inspired the saying "mind over matter." There'll be many times when you're in a location that prohibits your practicing (waiting for your turn to audition, for example). Perhaps this mental preparation will help you to reach your peak performance level. I can say from years of experience that it's helped me in my performances. Some athletes who have mentally practiced their sport throughout their careers include Michael Jordan, Nancy Kerrigan, and Jack Nicklaus. One book mentioned in the *Newsweek* article was *Mind Sculpture* by Ian Robertson.

Proverb 29: *Have fun*. I know—it sounds trite and is very hard to do, but approach each audition as an educational experience, and sooner or later your study will pay off.

4

"If You've Got Five Minutes I'll Teach You to Sing"

Randall Richardson

Have you ever seen advertisements that promise to teach you to play the piano or sing in an unbelievably short amount of time? That's not what this section is about. It's physically and mentally impossible to learn to sing well in five minutes, but this section should be beneficial to the unfortunate actor who can't find a voice teacher. Don't get discouraged if you have trouble grasping these ideas on singing. Professional singers train for years to master their voices. Just remember that any attempt you make to improve your voice will be rewarded by better singing.

The three areas related to vocal technique that I concentrate on most with my voice students are posture, breath control, and sound quality. These areas are interrelated and must operate at an efficient level and occur simultaneously in order to produce the best sound when you sing. Without good posture, the abdominal muscles, rib muscles, and diaphragm cannot maintain a coordinated control of the breath contained in the lungs. If breath control is not efficient, the throat muscles lock up, creating tension in the vocal mechanism, and the sound loses quality. Most actors work very hard to control the musculature that contributes to good sound when they speak, and singing has the same requirements but to a greater degree. As the pitch rises and falls, a singer must make certain adjustments in order to maintain the quality of sound that a trained speaking voice has.

Posture, breath control, and sound quality are taught and explained in many different ways. The following comments briefly touch on a few approaches that I have found useful in my voice teaching. I suggest that you study this chapter carefully before viewing the demonstrations contained on the accompanying website, because the information contained here and on the website will be very difficult to grasp with only one reading and viewing. You should revisit the material until you thoroughly understand the concepts and exercises.

Posture

Good posture requires that the spine remain long for the entire singing process. If your spine shortens, the chest collapses and changes the relationship of the muscles to each other. The breakdown in this relationship will result in inefficient breath control, which will greatly affect your singing. Maintaining a long spine (resembling a "noble" posture) while singing appears easy but becomes extremely difficult as you expend your air. My lessons with an Alexander Technique instructor have been very helpful to me and will be to you as well. You should check to see if one is in your area. It takes a great deal of practice to achieve a consistency in posture, but all effort is rewarded. To get started, try the following exercise:

1. In a standing position, lift your hands and arms over your head, and stretch for the ceiling while looking straight ahead.
2. Lower your hands and arms without lowering your upper torso, but at the same time relax your shoulders and arms. This is the posture you want. If it looks bad in a mirror, you're probably overdoing or underdoing it. Your posture should look "noble" but relaxed. Naturally, when you're on stage you need to assume many different postures, but the long spine concept can be incorporated into many bodily positions.
3. *Relax* is a word I use over and over in my teaching. If you try to do these exercises with upper body, throat, and jaw tension you won't accomplish much. The only tension you want in your body when you sing is the tension of the supporting muscles that will be discussed in the breath control section.

Breath Control

Breath control requires that you not only exhale properly but that you also inhale properly. In order to control the breath efficiently, you must combine the "noble" posture of the previous exercise with the breathing process.

1. Return to number 1 of the posture exercise and repeat it. While your hands and arms are above your head, relax your abdominal muscles and take several big breaths without lifting your chest any higher. You should feel your ribs and abdominal muscles expand when you do this. Next, lower your arms without lowering your torso and try to breathe the same way without heaving your chest higher (which should already be at the proper level if you've performed the posture exercise correctly). If you breathe like this when you perform, you'll be able to control the breath more efficiently, and you won't distract the audience with your heaving chest every time you breathe.

2. Once you've learned this technique of inhalation, you're ready to control the air a different way. The following exercises should help you to control your breath as you sing. Each exercise has the same goal, so after you've tried them all use the ones that help the most. I also suggest that you practice in front of a mirror as much as possible. Sometimes you will feel as if you are doing the exercise correctly but we humans tend to revert to habit and what feels natural. A mirror will help you to check your progress more objectively.

   • Relax your abdominal muscles, and take a breath that expands the area from your belt line to your sternum, including the ribs. My students do best at this when they imagine that they are only filling the bottom half of their lungs. Remember—relax your shoulders when you take your breath. Next, try to sing without any changes around this area of your abdomen. In other words, sing as if you're inhaling (or with the feeling of inhalation). The abdominal and rib muscles will tighten if you do this correctly

- Pretend that you've swallowed a balloon that extends all the way to your navel. The opening of the balloon is at your mouth. When you take a breath, the balloon fills with air from your navel to your sternum and ribs. As you sing don't let the balloon deflate where it expanded. Again—if you do this exercise correctly, the abdominal and rib muscles will tighten.
- Lay on your back. Cough or do a "belly laugh." Your abdominal muscles should tighten. After you've located the muscles that bounced when you coughed, and while you're still on your back, place a book on the muscles that bounced. As you sing, practice keeping the muscles tight (the book will lower gradually as your air is expended) the entire time.
- Sit on the edge of a chair with your chest collapsed, and bend over a little (not too much) with your arms between your legs. Take a breath as if you're filling the bottom half of the lungs. Do you feel your abdominal and rib muscles tighten? These are the same muscles that need to tighten when you sing.

I've noticed that when students begin to practice breathing they often draw one or two wrong conclusions. First, as they feel the tightness of the abdominal muscles involved in breath support, they mistakenly assume that it is like "sucking in the gut." The other misconception about breathing occurs when the singer feels the expansion of the ribs and abdominal area when she takes a breath. The expansion tricks her into thinking that breath support is accomplished by sticking out the stomach. Both misconceptions are very inefficient ways to control the breath, because they don't allow a balanced coordination of the singing muscles. Remember—relax the muscles to inhale and tense them to sing. The expansion you experience when you inhale will not increase or decrease when you tense the muscles to sing.

Sound Quality

Your voice can produce many types of sounds—bright, dark, nasal, throaty, and so on. The purpose of this section is to help you achieve a pleasing sound quality as you sing. Good sound quality will only be possible if your posture and breath control are correct. Otherwise, the muscles of the neck tense and greatly hinder a good sound. In other words, you need to replace tension in the throat with tension in the abdomen and rib muscles. Of the three components of singing, sound quality is the most difficult to learn by reading a book or watching a video; nevertheless, as with posture and breath control, even minimal effort is rewarded.

Actors work very hard on diction because diction is extremely important in a play. This emphasis on diction often works to an actor's disadvantage when singing is required, however, because they often try to sing with the same amount of space in the mouth and throat region that they have when they speak. Since singing is usually higher or lower in pitch than speech, the space in the mouth and throat region must change with the pitch. If the space doesn't change, the throat muscles tense, create a tense sound, and make the voice hard to maneuver. In spite of the necessity to have good diction, with a little work it's also possible to combine diction with good singing.

I find it interesting to teach both music majors who usually sing classical songs and theatre majors who usually sing musical theatre songs. The music majors generally have bad diction because much of their emphasis is on achieving a good tone. The theatre majors usually have great diction but have a poor tone as the range fluctuates. I always thought this was a mysterious phenomenon until discussing the problem with Don one day. He remarked that actors emphasize the consonants and singers emphasize the vowels. I suddenly realized that this was the reason my theatre students had trouble "opening up" their voices. As you practice the following exercises don't be afraid to "destroy" the diction for more openness. You won't really destroy the diction, but the extra space in your mouth will feel like it. Once you grasp the concept of singing with more openness, you can add the good diction back into the sound. This time, however, you want the diction (vowels and consonants) to feel as if it is in front of the space you've created—not in the throat. This will ensure that more of your sound will go where it belongs—to the audience.

In many vocal pedagogy books, singers are told to sing with a yawn. This is a very helpful concept because you must always have a certain amount of "high and low" space in the back of the mouth as you sing. The extra space encourages a relaxed open sound, but most people give this up too soon because they're unaccustomed to the space and are concerned that it will impair their diction. With practice, this yawn space will feel natural and have the added benefits of better sound as well as good diction. I suggest that you try the following exercises.

1. Sing with as much of a yawn as possible. Don't worry about diction. In fact, destroy the diction in favor of having a more relaxed throat and jaw. I tell my students to "sing dumb" as if they're actually yawning when trying this exercise. The object is to grow accustomed to having the soft palate higher and the throat relaxed.

2. When you feel that you're successful singing with the yawn space, it's time to practice incorporating diction with the open sound. Speak your name as if you're introducing yourself at an audition saying, "My name is . . ." (be careful that you don't raise the pitch of your voice). After doing this several times, realize that if you've introduced yourself with good sound quality and projection, you've achieved the same type of space in the mouth and throat region that you did when you practiced the yawn, but you added one more element. You projected the sound forward as all good actors do when they speak.

3. When you begin to understand and feel the type of mouth space and throat relaxation that you produce when you speak your name, you're ready for the next step. Pick a note that's not too high, and sing "My name is . . ." on the note,

trying to approximate the sound quality you had when you spoke your name. When you think you have the same type of sound quality as your speech, try singing in the same manner on higher and lower notes. Always remember that your throat will tense if you don't control the breath properly.

4. After you've mastered singing on one note, experiment with first speaking a phrase from a familiar song, singing the phrase on one note, and then singing the phrase as it is in the song. As you sing, try to project the sound as you do when you speak. Remember—in order to keep your speech quality when singing higher pitches, you must yawn more in the back of the mouth (as if there's an unbroken egg there and you don't want to crack it while you are singing) and keep the throat relaxed.

5. If the previous exercises have helped improve your sound quality, this last exercise might also prove helpful. By now, when you sing you should have a sensation of the sound resonating or originating in the mask of your face. If so, the following "crutch" or "gimmick" will help you to remember to keep it there as you practice.

   • Hold your hand (palm down) in front of your mouth with your top lip above and bottom lip below.

   • The goal will be to sing above the hand.

   • As you sing you want your throat to be relaxed (as if it's below the hand) at all times. As the pitch rises, you'll have the tendency to tighten the throat muscles. This will feel like you're pushing the throat upward and toward the hand. For the best sound quality, you want the throat to maintain the low, relaxed feeling it had when you practiced introducing yourself. If you're belting, it will be impossible to prevent the throat from pushing up toward the hand. Nevertheless, a little resistance to the pushing up will give the belt a fuller sound.

   • As you sing over the hand it might be helpful to think of singing with a smile on the inside of the mouth (above the hand). As the pitch rises, the smile lifts toward the eyes. As the smile lifts don't forget to control the breath correctly and to refrain from pushing the throat toward the hand. I tell my students to imagine a smile over the hand (in the sound) and a frown below the hand (in the throat).

Don't be impatient if you don't see instant improvement in your singing, although there often is. It is difficult to change muscular habits, and you've been speaking and singing the same way for many years. The best way to improve and to continue improving is to practice these basic exercises every day and every time you sing. Consistency is the key to improvement.

Belting

I would be remiss if I didn't say a few words about belting. As a voice teacher who was trained to sing in the classical style, I can relate to those voice teachers who avoid belting like the plague, and who make a cross with their fingers as if warding off vampires. My early professional life was spent looking down my nose at singers who belt; however, I began to realize that when I sang higher than usual in my chest voice, I was actually belting. Although belting occurs sporadically in classical singing, it's so prevalent in musical theatre that it's stylistically incorrect to omit it in many songs. Belting is expected in Broadway shows because the range of many songs is written in the lower range of the woman's voice (C^3–C^4, consult the range chart in the user's guide for song excerpts). Women must belt in order to have a stronger sound, and it makes their diction more natural. In men's voices, belting is less prevalent but occurs when the music is in their upper range and they resist flipping over into their head voice.

If you're planning to have a career that will require belting in performances on a daily schedule (as on Broadway), it's very important to learn to belt healthily. If you don't, you could eventually ruin your voice. Unfortunately, you never know if belting incorrectly will ruin your voice until it's too late. Some voices can belt incorrectly for years and never show any wear or tear, and some voices can belt incorrectly for a short period of time and develop nodules or other vocal problems. I often tell my students that voices are like automobiles. When you buy a new, shiny one off the lot you don't know whether it will be a great car or a lemon. Since you don't know the amount of endurance your voice will have, it's necessary that you sing as correctly as possible.

One of the most common problems experienced by young singers in auditions is their choice of when to belt and when to mix the lower and upper voice together (belt mix). The wrong decision usually prohibits the voice from operating at maximum efficiency. Some singers can belt higher than others, and it's very important that you know how high you can carry the belt before mixing it with the upper voice. If you carry the belt higher than you should, pitch and sound quality usually deteriorate. In a way, the voice is like a manual transmission in a car (that's right—another car analogy). You can drive pretty fast (or sing pretty high) in first gear, but as your speed increases you need to shift gears in order to continue to accelerate (or sing higher). If you don't shift gears, the car (or voice) will not hit its maximum speed (you'll sing flat), and it will probably begin to experience some damage if driven like this continuously. Similarly, your voice needs to shift at certain points in the range or it could begin to develop physical problems.

I strongly recommend that you find a teacher who can instruct you on how to belt healthily. Learning to belt well is a difficult process, and it's best learned with a teacher. If there's no teacher in your town to help you, look in other towns within driving distance. Unfortunately, our ears do not hear our voices as well as other people's ears do. Even though I've been singing professionally for over thirty-two years, it's still helpful to have another set of ears to hear me. So, three or four times a year I drive two hundred miles to take a maintenance lesson with my voice teacher. If you look everywhere and still can't find a teacher, maybe these suggestions will help:

Control Your Breath
In all types of singing, good breath control is extremely important. This is especially true when you belt. Think back on the

example I gave about the car's manual transmission (I promise—the last car analogy). The faster the car goes in first gear, the more gas it needs to maintain its speed. Belting is a lot like this. You are singing higher than your voice normally goes without shifting into the upper voice, so it needs all the gas (or breath control) that you can muster to maintain the higher notes. It also requires more air, since you'll be singing louder in your belt voice.

Relax Your Throat

As the pitch ascends in a voice that's belting, the throat will tighten. This will make the voice less flexible and will tend to produce a squeezed sound. While throat tension goes along with belting, the more you try to relax the throat, the better sound quality you'll have. Again, good breath control is needed to help keep the throat muscles as relaxed as possible.

Put the Sound in the Nose

This doesn't mean that you should sing nasally, although some belters do. Instead, you should try to put the sound in the nose area (the mask of the face), especially as the range increases toward the high belt. I believe the famous voice teacher Jean de Reszke once said, "The sound should be in the nose, but not the nose in the sound." When you belt, you want your sound to be bright and as far forward as you can get it (you might want to refer back to the section on sound quality). You should also remember that your purpose for singing and speaking are to communicate the words and the words should always be forward. If they're in the throat they're not going out to the audience. The forwardness of the sound will also help you to keep the throat more relaxed.

Listen to the Best

It's hard to find something if you don't know where it is. Conversely, learning to belt correctly is difficult if you can't imagine the type of sound you want to produce. You need to listen to recordings of good belters and empathize with their singing. I often have my students listen to a recording with their eyes closed while they pay close attention to where the sound seems to be originating. After the student empathizes with the singer on the recording for a while, I ask them to keep their eyes closed and to sing like the singer on the recording. This often creates immediate improvement. A good belter's sound will seem to be forward most of the time. If the belter's sound is throaty, gravelly, or raspy, I wouldn't use her as a role model.

Appendix A
A Listing of Selected Combined Auditions

Illinois Theatre Association
Contact:
1225 W. Belmont Ave.
Chicago, IL 60657-3205
Website: http://members.aol.com/iltheassoc/ProAud.html
Fee: $30
The Audition: The acting audition will be three minutes and feature two contrasting monologues. A musical audition will be four minutes and feature two monologues and sixteen bars from a song.
Special Considerations: The application deadline is mid-February with an audition date in early March. This audition is open to students enrolled in Illinois colleges and universities or to college and university students who are planning a move to Chicago, and to freelance, non-union actors. A committee of professional actors and directors and representatives from the League of Chicago Theatres and the Illinois Theatre Association conducts a preliminary screening audition. Final callback auditions are held a day after the preliminaries.

Indiana Theatre Association
Contact:
106 Poplar Street
Greencastle, IN 46135
Ph: (765) 658-6509
e-mail: intheatre@netdirect.net
Website: http://www.intheatre.org/auditions.html
Fee: $20

The Audition: You will have two minutes total for a song or a song and a monologue.

Special Considerations: This audition has a mid-February deadline for a late February audition. This audition is for actors seeking summer and year-round, paid acting positions. Applications are accepted from union and non-union actors. Non-union applicants and applicants with limited professional experience must be recommended by a professional director or a director working in academia.

Midwest Theatre Auditions

Contact:
Webster University
470 E. Lockwood
St. Louis, MO 63119-3194
Ph: (314) 968-6937
Fax: (314) 963-6048
e-mail: mwt@pop.webster.edu
Website: http://www.websteruniv.edu/depts/finearts/theatre /mwta
Fee: $25

The Audition: You will have ninety seconds for a monologue or a monologue and a song. Those who sing are requested to sing first.

Special Considerations: This audition has a mid-December application deadline for an audition date in mid-February. Applications are accepted from Equity and non-Equity performers looking for paid positions in summer stock theatres, outdoor dramas, Shakespeare festivals, college and professional training programs and internships.

National Dinner Theatre Association

Contact:
P.O. Box 726
Marshall, MI 49068
Ph: (616) 781-7859
Fax: (616) 781-4880
Website: http://www.ndta.com/ndtahome.html

The website acts as a clearinghouse for local auditions. Check the site for information about auditions nationwide or write directly to the home office for an application.

New England Theatre Conference
Contact:
Northeastern University Dept. of Theatre
360 Huntington Ave.
Boston, MA 02115
Ph: (617) 424-9275
Fax: (617) 424-1057
e-mail: NETC@world.std.com
Website: http://netconline.org/auditions/auditions.html
Fees: All applicants must pay an application and processing fee. The fee for current NETC members is $30. For nonmembers, audition fees are $45 for students and $50 for nonstudents.
The Audition: The NETC audition allows two minutes for the performer. The NETC does have a resume screening prior to the final audition.
Special Considerations: This audition has an application deadline of late January for an audition date in mid-March. NETC accepts applications from non-Equity performers and college students. NETC is not open to Equity members, high school students, or anyone under eighteen years old. All applicants become NETC members, and the fee is nonrefundable. However, applicants who are not selected for an audition slot will have their application/resume information forwarded to the casting people who do hire directly from the applications. Seventy or more producers, talent agents, and representatives from training institutes will audition prescreened applicants. Approximately 750 of over 1,000 applicants are given appointments for an audition.

New Jersey Theatre Group
Contact:
17 Cook Ave.
Madison, NJ 07940

Ph: (973) 593-0189
Fax: (973) 377-4842
Website: http://www.nj.com/njtheatre/
The NJTG is an alliance of professional, Equity theatres. Year-round auditions are posted on the website by the theatre. Equity and non-Equity auditions are held in mid-February and August. For more information, contact the New Jersey Theatre Group directly.

Northwest Drama Conference Auditions
Contact:
University of Idaho-Moscow
Theatre Arts Department
Moscow, ID 83844-3074
Ph: (208) 885-6197
Fax: (208) 885-2558
The Audition: Actors are allowed four minutes to display contrasting monologues and a song.
Fees: The fee is $45 for students and $75 for nonstudents plus a $10 registration fee.
Special Considerations: This audition has a late January application deadline for a mid-February audition date. These auditions are for admission to graduate school programs in the northwestern and western United States, and for regional summer theatres.

Ohio Theatre Alliance
Contact:
Franciscan University
1235 University Blvd.
Steubenville, OH 43952
Ph: (740) 537-5178
Website: http://www.ohiotheatrealliance.org
/ohiotheatrealliance/annual_auditions.html
Fee: $35
The Audition: You will have ninety seconds to perform a monologue or a monologue and a song. If you wish to sing you must provide taped accompaniment.

Special Considerations: This audition has a mid-January application deadline for an early February audition date. This audition is open to Equity and non-Equity actors and student actors, eighteen years or older. The organization is especially trying to attract actors twenty-one and older. Companies offer positions in summer stock, year-round employment, paying and nonpaying, graduate/training programs, apprenticeships, internships, touring groups, children's theatre, and outdoor drama.

National Outdoor Drama Auditions
Contact:
Institute of Outdoor Drama
CB #3240 1700 Airport Road
University of North Carolina
Chapel Hill, NC 27599-3240
Ph: (919) 962-1328
Website: http://www.unc.edu/depts/outdoor
Fees: $30 or $25 for University of North Carolina students.
The Audition: Acting, singing, and dance auditions are held separately. You will have one minute for your monologue and one minute for your song and be asked to learn a brief dance progression.
Special Considerations: This audition has an early March application deadline for a mid-March audition date. You must be at least eighteen years old to audition. You must have previous experience in theatre and be available for the entire summer. Outdoor dramas are often lavishly staged costume and music pieces with an emphasis on the sweep of history. The casts are large and need actors with strong voices for speaking and singing. Dance skills are a big plus. Performers with stunt, stage combat, and horseback skills also receive strong consideration.

Southeastern Theatre Conference
Contact:
P.O. Box 9868
Greensboro, NC 27429-0868
Ph: (336) 272-3645

Website: http://www.setc.org/

Fees: Must be paid by money order for $115 (professional adults) or $55 (student), which includes audition fee, registration, and membership.

Special Considerations: SETC has an early February application deadline for professionals and an October deadline for students for an early March audition date. SETC specifically discourages performance of Shakespeare, dialect pieces, and pieces containing profanity or sexually explicit language. Auditions are for Equity and non-Equity actors and dancers seeking professional, summer, and full-time, paid positions with professional companies. Many apprentice positions are also available. Students wishing to audition at the spring conference must audition at the state level and pass an initial phase of callbacks. For nonstudents to attain an audition slot you must not be enrolled in school, be available to work full time, have worked professionally on two occasions, and list your credits on the professional audition form. Non-Equity actors must have a signed reference from a professional director verifying your work.

California Educational Theatre Association
Contact:
CETA Auditions, Buddy Butler, Coordinator
Theatre Arts Department
San Jose State University
San Jose, CA 95192
Ph: (408) 924-4557
Website: http://www.cetaweb.org

Fees: $15 plus $30 fee from participating schools.

The Audition: You will have four minutes for two monologues or one monologue and a song.

Special Considerations: This audition has a late January application deadline for a mid-February audition. Participants are from California, Nevada, Arizona, Utah, Hawaii, Guam, and other western states. Preliminary auditions screen applicants for the finals. Recruiters may attend preliminaries as well as finals.

Southwest Theatre Association
Contact:
Southwest Theatre Association
3000 General Pershing Boulevard
Oklahoma City, OK 73107
Website: http://www.southwest-theater.com/SWTA2.html
Fees: $20 for SWTA members, $60 for nonmembers, $35 for student nonmembers.
The Audition: You will have ninety seconds plus sixteen bars if you choose to sing. Companies offer positions in summer stock, year-round employment, paying and nonpaying, graduate/training programs, apprenticeships, internships, touring groups, children's theatre, and outdoor drama.

StrawHat Auditions
Contact:
1771 Post Road East, Suite 315
Westport, CT 06880
Website: http://www.strawhat-auditions.com/who.htm
Fees: $65 includes use of the internet portfolio and placement service.
The Audition: You will have one minute for a monologue and an additional minute for a song.
Special Considerations: These auditions take place in late March in New York City. The application deadline is in February. StrawHat is open to non-Equity and Equity-eligible actors looking to start and continue their professional careers in the theatre. Dancers, singers, actors of all types, sizes, genders, and nationality are encouraged to apply. Most auditions are for summer stock theatres although some Equity theatres seeking Membership Candidates and interns also attend and can offer year-round opportunities. Around five hundred performing positions are generally available.

Theatre Bay Area General Auditions
Contact:
657 Mission St., Ste. 402

San Francisco, CA 94105
Ph: (414) 957-1557
Fax: (415) 957-1556
Website: http://www.theatrebayarea.org/genaud01.html

Fees: No fees listed but very limited admission. This audition provides about three hundred slots for about seven hundred applicants. Non-Equity actors must be Theatre Bay Area members. The membership fee is approximately $40 per year.

Audition: You will have two minutes as a non-Equity actor and three minutes as an Equity actor.

Special Considerations: This audition has a mid-December application deadline for a late February audition date. Non-Equity actors must also fulfill *one* of the following requirements for consideration:

- have accumulated the equivalent of one year of full-time acting training
- be an Equity Membership Candidate (contact Equity to find out about the Membership Candidate program)
- have proof of performance in at least six, nonschool stage productions

Actors of color, physically challenged actors, and actors under eighteen years or over fifty years are encouraged to apply.

Unified Professional Theatre Auditions
Contact:
Playhouse on the Square
51 S. Cooper St.
Memphis, TN 38104
Ph: (901) 725-0776
Fax: (901) 272-7530

Fee: $30

Audition: You will have ninety seconds for a monologue or a monologue and a song.

Special Considerations: This audition has a late December application deadline for an early February audition date. This audition is for performers seeking paid, year-round positions and paid internships. To audition you must be available for employment throughout the year, not just the summer, and not planning on returning to school. You must also meet at least one of the following requirements:

- have a post-graduate theatre degree
- have your registration signed by a registered UPTA (Unified Professional Theatre Auditions) theatre
- have your registration signed by a Theatre Communications Group (TCG) member theatre
- have attended a previous UPTA audition
- be a member of Equity or of the Equity Membership Candidate Program

University/Resident Theatre Association (U/RTA) National Unified Auditions
Contact:
1560 Broadway, Ste. 414
New York, NY 10036
Ph: (212) 221-1130
Fax (212) 869-2752
Website: http://www.urta.com/
Fees: $70 paid by cashiers check, money order, or credit card. The fee is nonrefundable.
The Audition: This audition has a late November application deadline for three audition dates. Auditions are held in Irvine, California, in early February; Chicago in mid-February; and New York City in late February. You will have three minutes to perform contrasting monologues and an additional thirty seconds to perform sixteen bars if you choose to sing. If you sing you will need to provide your own taped accompaniment and a player. The Irvine audition does not require the actors to pass a screening audition. The New York and Chicago auditions do.
Special Considerations: These auditions are designed for graduating seniors who are seeking graduate school admission. Several hundred positions are offered annually, primarily through acceptance to M.F.A. programs. The Master Audition Program is for Master of Fine Arts candidates about to graduate, or who have graduated in the preceding two years.

Graduation from a U/RTA member program is required. Select graduates will audition for casting directors, agents, and other representatives from participating professional theatre organizations.

Appendix B
User's Guide to the Website—Monologues

The monologue directory on the website <heinemanndrama
.com/auditionsourcebook> is not meant to substitute for the
reading of plays. The directory should serve as a guide to a wide
range of plays from a number of authors with some specific suggestions on where you may look to find a monologue you could
use in your audition. Each entry will provide specific information to help you in your search for the right monologue.

Title, Author, and Translator

This entry will provide you an initial starting point as you look
for a particular play. Plays originally written in languages other
than English may be available in several different English trans-
lations. We have recommended some versions we think work
well for contemporary actors.

Publisher

This entry should help you if you wish to purchase the recommended play. Also, classic and period works are frequently
available from more than one publisher. We are referencing a
particular version from a particular publisher. The publisher we
list simply reflects the version we are most familiar with.

Character, Age, and Gender

This entry will help you identify exactly which monologue we
are recommending and whether or not the monologue is appropriate for your consideration.

Mood, Time Period, and Locale

This entry is a limited introduction to the play's given circumstances provided to pique your interest and give you some sense of the monologue's language and performance requirements.

Cultural Considerations

This entry will provide specific information for those who may need a monologue for a culturally specific audition. Most entries are proposed as neutral with the belief that fine acting transcends race. We do wish to recognize that certain works speak to the cultural heritage and experience of a more focused community.

Length

This entry is not meant to be prescriptive, but rather an estimation of how long this monologue may run under typical conditions. Pace and delivery will vary from actor to actor and can result in a wide variance in performance length. You will need to work out your pace and timing with your coach. ' = minutes and " = seconds.

First Line and Last Line

These entries are accompanied by a page number or, as in the case of works with multiple versions or publishers, an act or scene reference. This information should help you locate the monologues we recommend from the particular play. We strongly urge you to read the play, however. You may find in your reading a monologue that will work even better for you than those we recommend. The key is to find the right monologue, whatever it takes.

Sample Monologue Entries

1940s Radio Hour, The/Walton Jones

Publisher/Rights Distributor:	Samuel French, Inc.
Character/Age/Gender/Cultural Considerations:	Geneva/20s–30s/Female/Neutral/
Mood/Time/Locale:	Comedy/1940s/Radio Broadcast Studio
Length:	45"
First Line:	p. 29. "Last night, Curtis and Izzy and I . . ."
Last Line:	". . . she was pretending that she knew me."

Amy's View/David Hare

Publisher/Rights Distributor:	Samuel French, Inc.
Character/Age/Gender/Cultural Considerations:	Amy/Female/Neutral/20s
Mood/Time/Locale:	Melodrama/Contemporary/ England
Length:	1'
First Line:	p. 34. "The truth is . . ."
Last Line:	"So you see this must make things difficult."

Extremities/William Mastrosimone

Publisher/Rights Distributor:	Smith and Krauss/William Mastrosimone *Collected Plays*
Character/Age/Gender/Cultural Considerations:	Marjorie/Late 20s/Female/ Neutral
Mood/Time/Locale:	Melodrama/Contemporary/ Female/Neutral
Length:	2'15"
First Line:	p. 128. "Police. Charges. Arraignment."
Last Line:	"He's never leaving this house."

Italian American Reconciliation/John Patrick Shanley

Publisher/Rights Distributor:	Applause/13 by Shanley
Character/Age/Gender/Cultural Considerations:	Aldo/Late 20s/Male/Neutral
Mood/Time/Locale:	Comic, Ironic/Contemporary/ New York
Length:	1'
First Line:	p. 266. "You're right."
Last Line:	"Promising yourself into a country without a constitution."

Merchant of Venice, The/William Shakespeare

Publisher/Rights Distributor:	Addison-Wesley Pub. Co./*The Complete Works of Shakespeare*
Character/Age/Gender/Cultural Considerations:	Shylock/Late 40s or 50s/Male/Neutral
Mood/Time/Locale:	Melodramatic, Angry/ Elizabethan/Italy
Length:	1' 20"
First Line:	III.iii. "If it will feed nothing else . . ."
Last Line:	". . . but I will better the instruction."

Appendix C

User's Guide to the Website—Song Excerpts

Title

The song title will be in bold.

Musical

The musical (or large work) that contains the song will be in italics.

Composer/Lyricist

The composer is listed first/the lyricist is listed second.

Voice Part

Soprano, Mezzo-Soprano/Belter, Tenor, and Bass–Baritone. Most songs are classified by range. Often a tenor will sing a high baritone song, or a mezzo-soprano will sing a soprano song. I suggest that you look through all the entries for your sex if you have trouble finding an excerpt in your specific voice classification.

Cultural Considerations

This category indicates the ethnicity of the character singing the song. The categories to search for are Neutral (any nationality), African American, Asian, Jewish, and Hispanic.

Musical Source

This category gives the title of the vocal collection, vocal selection book, vocal score, or movie.

Distributor

The distributor of the vocal collection is given here. If the distributor is not known, the publisher is given.

Range

The range is the distance from the lowest note to the highest note in the excerpt. Middle C is C^3.

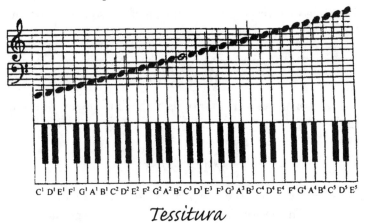

Tessitura

Tessitura refers to the part of the range that includes a majority of the notes. The categories to search are L = Low, ML = Medium Low, M = Medium, MH = Medium High, and H = High. In order

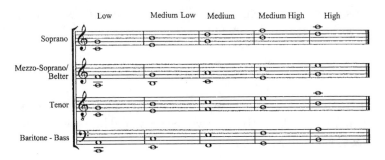

to give a better description of the tessitura in some songs, more than one letter (M–MH, L–ML, MH–H, etc.) is given.

Tempo

This category indicates the speed of the song excerpt. Categories to search are S = Slow, MS = Moderately Slow, M = Moderate, MF = Moderately Fast, and F = Fast. When a song excerpt has more than two tempos, the different tempos will be separated by a slash (M/F, S/F, MS/M, etc.).

Description

This category gives a brief description of the song style (example: bouncy, lyrical, swing style, etc.).

Song Plot

This category gives a brief synopsis of the dramatic event inspiring the song.

Measures

This category allows the searcher to locate the song excerpt in the music. The measures are numbered from the beginning of the song to the end (partial measures are counted as one measure unless they are completed during the introduction of the song). Whenever there are multiple endings or a coda, the count continues through the longest ending to the end of the song. Repeat signs are not observed. The ending to be sung will be noted in parenthesis (example: 34–56(2)) if clarification is needed.

Key

This category gives the key of the song excerpt. In excerpts that are in multiple keys, the keys will be separated by a slash (example: C Major/F Major/G Major).

Excerpt Length

This category gives the length of the song excerpt in seconds.
" = Seconds.

Sample Song Excerpt Entries

Ain't No Party (*Dreamgirls*), Henry Krieger/Tom Egen

Voice Part:	Soprano
Cultural Considerations:	African American
Musical Source:	*Vocal Selections*
Distributor:	Warner Bros. Publications
Range: F^3–F^4	*Tessitura:* M *Tempo:* M
Description:	Lyrical
Song Plot:	Lorrell sings of how hard it is to be in love with a married man.
Measures: 9–33	*Key:* F Major *Excerpt Length:* 33"

Art Is Calling for Me (*Enchantress, The*), Victor Herbert/Harry B. Smith

Voice Part:	Soprano
Cultural Considerations:	Neutral
Musical Source:	*The Singer's Musical Theatre Anthology, Soprano,* vol. 2
Distributor:	Hal Leonard Corporation
Range: G^3–G^4	*Tessitura:* MH *Tempo:* MF
Description:	Lyrical, requires facile articulation
Song Plot:	All she wants to do is sing on the stage.
Measures: 63–77	*Key:* E^b Major *Excerpt Length:* 18"

Hold On (*Secret Garden, The*), Lucy Simon/Marsha Norman

Voice Part:	Mezzo-Soprano/Belter
Cultural Considerations:	Neutral
Musical Source:	*The Singer's Musical Theatre Anthology, Mezzo-Soprano/Belter,* vol. 2
Distributor:	Hal Leonard Corporation
Range: F^2–B^3	*Tessitura:* L *Tempo:* M
Description:	Speech-like, dramatic
Song Plot:	Martha encourages Mary to be courageous in the face of adversity.
Measures: 6–24	*Key:* D Major *Excerpt Length:* 35"

77

Agony (*Into the Woods*), Stephen Sondheim
Voice Part:	Tenor
Cultural Considerations:	Neutral
Musical Source:	*Vocal Selections*
Distributor:	Warner Bros. Publications
Range: D^3–F^4	*Tessitura:* MH *Tempo:* M
Description:	Lyrical
Song Plot:	Rapunzel's Prince is frustrated by Rapunzel's predicament.
Measures: 18–36	*Key:* F Major *Excerpt Length:* 30"

Meditation II (*Shenandoah*), Gary Geld/Peter Udell
Voice Part:	Bass-Baritone
Cultural Considerations:	Neutral
Musical Source:	*Vocal Selections*
Distributor:	Hal Leonard Corporation
Range: C^3–E^4	*Tessitura:* MH *Tempo:* MF/MS
Description:	Dramatic, lyrical
Song Plot:	Charlie tells his deceased wife that the answer to all the fighting is found in the cemeteries.
Measures: 22–37	*Key:* F Minor *Excerpt Length:* 33"

Bibliography

Auditioning

Alper, S. M. 1995. *Next! Auditioning for the Musical Theatre*. Portsmouth, NH: Heinemann.

A good book for learning about the different types of musical theatre auditions. Contains great stories to illustrate suggestions and good information on music preparation.

Black, D., and E. Wallach. 1990. *The Actor's Audition*. New York: Vintage Books.

This book is most valuable for the advice it offers on approaches to the cold reading audition and the insight it gives on mental preparation for the audition experience.

Cohen, R. 1998. *Acting Professionally*. Fifth edition. Mountain View, CA: Mayfield.

Perhaps the best book available today on the subject of acting as a career. Cohen is occasionally harsh in his presentation of the facts and dismissive to the point of being elitist in his discussion of actor training programs. Aside from these flaws this book is a must-have for any aspiring actor.

Craig, D. 1990. *On Singing Onstage*. New York: Applause.

Helpful dos and don'ts section. Good section on how to perform a song. Some information about judges in an audition.

Craig, D. 1993. *A Performer Prepares: A Guide to Song Preparation for Actors, Singers and Dancers*. New York: Applause.

Very good source for useful information on song interpretation. Covers different styles; ballad, up-tempo, showstopper, blues, etc. Lists representative songs in each style. Written as a conversation between a vocal coach and a singer.

Eaker, S. 1989. *The Back Stage Handbook for Performing Artists*. New York: Back Stage Books.

A very helpful book for the performer who is about to make the jump from amateur to professional. The sections "Basic Tools" and "Training" are particularly helpful for the young actor anticipating a career in theatre.

Ellis, R. 1986. *An Audition Handbook for Student Actors*. Chicago: Nelson-Hall.

Contains good suggestions on selecting and preparing audition material.

Fineburgh, N., and A. McArthur. 1993 *Hot Tips for Cold Readings: Some Do's and Don'ts for Actors at Auditions*. Louisville, KY: Smith and Kraus.

This book offers some solid pointers on the art of the cold read. The authors have a good insight into the actor-director relationship.

Friedman, G. H. 1996. *Call-Back: How to Prepare for the Call-Back to Succeed in Getting the Part*. New York: Limelight Editions.

Helpful hints for succeeding in callback auditions.

Friedman, G. H. 1998. *The Perfect Monologue: How to Find and Perform the Monologue That Will Get You the Part*. New York: Limelight Editions.

Offers insights from a veteran casting director on selecting and composing an audition monologue. This book is worth a look.

Funk, B. 1996. *The Audition Process: A Practical Guide for Actors*. Portsmouth, NH: Heinemann.

For the college or high school actor, this book is a great place to start. This is an easy-to-read, commonsense text on what to expect out of the audition process. Bob Funk treats his reader with civility and respect and this makes the advice much more palatable.

Haber, M., with B. Babchick. 1999. *How to Get the Part Without Falling Apart*. Los Angeles: Lone Eagle.

Quite a few audition stories by well-known actors talking about audition experiences (some good and some bad). Many helpful hints on preparing for the audition.

Hoffman, B. 1999. *Cold Reading and How to Be Good at It.* Toluca Lake, CA: Dramaline.
This is probably the best book on the market right now on the subject of cold reading. Since the cold read is the final hurdle for most casting directors, this book should be on your shelf or, better still, by your nightstand if you want to act.

Hooks, E. 1996. *The Audition Book.* New York: Back Stage Books.
Good audition information. Useful audition checklist.

Howard, G. 2000. *Casting Director's Secrets.* New York: Allworth Press.
This is the latest offering from a respected authority on the audition. Common sense tells us that if she is one of the best we better listen to what she says. This is a book to consider.

Hunt, G. 1995. *How to Audition: For TV, Movies, Commercials, Plays and Musicals.* New York: Harper Perennial.
Good book for all types of auditions. Analyzes the process and gives many helpful hints. Features chapters in question/answer format with a number of successful people in the business—Stephen Sondheim, Hal Prince, Richard Rodgers, etc.

Kanner, E., P. G. Bens, and P. G. Bens Jr. 1997. *Next: An Actor's Guide to Auditioning.* Hollywood, CA: Lone Eagle.
This book is highly regarded by professionals for the savvy and common sense it provides for actors starting their careers.

Kondazian, E. S., and R. Dreyfuss. 2000. *The Actor's Encyclopedia of Casting Directors: Conversations with over 100 Casting Directors on How to Get the Job.* Hollywood, CA: Lone Eagle.
This book is essential for actors considering a career in film or television. The sheer volume of inside wisdom may seem

overwhelming, even discouraging. But this is the owner's manual for your film career.

Oliver, D. 1985. *How to Audition for the Musical Theatre: A Step-by-Step Guide to Effective Preparation*. North Stratford, NH: Smith and Kraus.
Good preparation book. Contains a useful section on selecting audition material.

Peithman, S., and N. Offen, ed. 1999. *The Stage Directions Guide to Auditions*. Portsmouth, NH: Heinemann.
A good book for some dos and don'ts of auditioning. Also includes information on combating stage fright, tips from a college recruiter, resumes, headshots, and tips on warming up.

Searle, J. 1995. *Getting the Part: Thirty-Three Professional Casting Directors Tell You How to Get Work in Theatre, Films, Commercials, and TV*. New York: Limelight Editions.
Do not overlook this commonsense look at the audition from the professional perspective. This book is useful for actors who have completed their education and are ready to start their career.

Shurtleff, M., and B. Fosse. 1980. *Audition*. New York: Bantam.
This book remains the standard by which all audition books are measured. If you do not have a copy, get one. Today.

Silver, F. 1985. *Auditioning for the Musical Theatre*. New York: Penguin Books.
Includes a section on what to sing in auditions, a small, useful compendium of possible audition songs, and suggestions on how to succeed in the sixteen-bar audition. Helpful section explaining the difference between a vocal coach and a voice teacher.

Silverberg, L. 1996. *Loving to Audition: The Audition Workbook for Actors*. Louisville, KY: Smith and Kraus.
This is a very fine, very detailed textbook on approaching the audition monologue text and converting it to performance. Silverberg analyzes two monologues in exacting detail and illustrates exactly how to make the monologue your own.

Headshot/Resumé

Charles, J., and T. Bloom. 1991. *The Actor's Picture/Resumé Book: An Actor's Guide to Creating a Picture/Resumé for Theatre, Film, and Commercials.* Dorset, VT: Theatre Directories.
An excellent book devoted entirely to headshots and resumes. Read this book before you have pictures made.

Performance Anxiety

Brebner, A. 1990. *Setting Free the Actor.* San Francisco, CA: Mercury House.
This is a self-help book that works. This book is brimming with insight on the actor's life and how to sustain balance and perspective.

Dunkel, S. E. 1989. *The Audition Process: Anxiety Management and Coping Strategies.* New York: Pendragon Press.
Although written by someone who has auditioned for symphony orchestras, the book is applicable to all areas of performance. The author's ideas on what to eat before an audition and his "audition bag" contents are particularly interesting.

Green, B., with W. T. Gallwey. 1986. *The Inner Game of Music.* New York: Doubleday.
Timothy Gallwey's ideas on performance anxiety have been accepted for a long time, and in this book Barry Green applies them to performing music. Although this book is written with the classical artist in mind, the concepts apply to all performers.

Robertson, I. H. 2000. *Mind Sculpture: Unlocking Your Brain's Untapped Potential.* New York: Fromm International.

Songs

DeVenney, D. P. 1998. *The Broadway Song Companion: An Annotated Guide to Musical Literature by Voice Type and Song Style.* Lanham, MD: Scarecrow Press.

Annotated catalogue of songs, duets, trios, etc. found in over two hundred musicals. Annotation includes composer, lyricist, character's name, voice type, range, and song style. The book also contains nine helpful indices.

Voice

Berry, C. 1973. *Voice and the Actor*. New York: Macmillan.
Deals with producing sound on a holistic basis. Good exercises and photos with many monologues for practice. Good diction section.

Linklater, K. 1976. *Freeing the Natural Voice*. New York: Drama.
Good book about freeing the voice and body of tension that prohibits maximum efficiency. Contains some good exercises and concepts dealing with producing good sound quality.

Robison, K. 2000. *The Actor Sings: Discovering a Musical Voice for the Stage*. Portsmouth, NH: Heinemann.
A good commonsense book about the vocal mechanism and how to sing well. There is also a helpful chapter on the articulators that are involved in producing good diction.

Young, A. H. 1995. *Singing Professionally: Studying Singing for Actors and Singers*. Portsmouth, NH: Heinemann.
A helpful book divided into sections for beginning, intermediate, and advanced singers. The section "Zen in the Art of Singing" is particularly thought-provoking.

Ordering Music

Listed below are Internet addresses of music dealers. If you need music quickly call a music dealer on the phone in order to ascertain the availability of the music you want. Some of the Internet sites don't tell you if music is in stock. If you have a music dealer order music you might have a long wait.

Online Sites

www.amazon.com
www.broadwaynewyork.com
www.colonymusic.com (Colony Records, New York City)
www.bn.com (Barnes and Noble)
www.pianospot.com
www.encoremusic.com
www.sheetmusicplus.com (Sheet Music Plus, Syracuse)
www.penders.com (Penders Music Company, Texas and
   Oklahoma)
www.jwpepper.com (J.W. Pepper & Company, Atlanta)
www.brodtmusic.com (Brodt Music, North Carolina)

Phone Numbers of Music Dealers

Colony Records	(New York City)	(212) 265-1260
Sheet Music Plus	(Syracuse)	(315) 428-9225
T.I.S. Music Shop	(Indiana)	(800) 421-8132
Penders Music Company	(Texas and Oklahoma)	(800) 772-5918
J.W. Pepper & Sons	(Atlanta)	(800) 345-6296
Brodt Music	(North Carolina)	(800) 438-4129
Stanton's Sheet Music Inc.	(Ohio)	(800) 426-8742
Schmitt Music Company	(Minneapolis)	(800) 767-3434

Malechi Music Company	(Michigan)	(800) 253-9692
	(California)	(800) 858-7664
	(Washington)	(800) 541-2001
	(Iowa)	(800) 831-4197